BASIC
TRAINING
A MANUAL FOR
TEENS

Gospel Advocate
Nashville, Tennessee

BASIC
TRAINING
A MANUAL FOR
TEENS

Thirteen Basic
Bible Teachings
That *You* Need
To Know

RANDY SIMMONS

Published by Gospel Advocate Co.
P.O. Box 150, Nashville, TN 37202
http://www.gospeladvocate.com

ISBN: 0-89225-390-8

DEDICATION

To my wonderful church family,
Gulf Coast Church of Christ, Fort Myers, Fla.

Table of Contents

INTRODUCTION

Parris Island, S.C., home of the Marine Corps Recruit Depot, where Marines are made.

Your local church teen Sunday school class, where Christians are made.

At first glance, the two may seem to have little in common, but in reality they have much in common.

Parris Island is the birthplace of basically trained Marines. It is where Marines are forged in a furnace of shared hardship and tough training. It is where beliefs are formed and character is developed. Marine Corps recruits are trained physically, mentally and morally. Their proudly stated basic values are honor, courage and commitment.

The mission of the local church Sunday school class or youth group is very similar. It is the primary classroom for basically trained Christians. It is where eternally important beliefs are taught and spiritual training is encouraged. It is a place where bonds of friendship are created so that young Christians can go forward together with commitment to Christ.

In my first book, *Straight Talk for Teens*, we looked at moral issues facing teenagers. In my second book, *What to Do When You Don't Know What to Do*, we discussed personal and emotional issues facing teenagers. Now, in *Basic Training: A Manual for Teens,* we will be looking at basic beliefs in Scripture that should be a part of every Christian teen's faith experience.

What are those basic beliefs? What is basic training for Christian teens? To answer that question, I asked myself two questions: "What do I want my own children to know about God, Jesus, the Bible and the church?" and "What do I want the teenagers in my church to know about those same subjects?" I wanted to address questions like:

- How do we know the Bible is true?
- What is God like?
- What is my relationship to Jesus Christ?
- Who is the Holy Spirit, and what difference does He make in my life?
- How can I have stronger faith?
- Is baptism essential for salvation?
- Why do we partake of the Lord's Supper each Sunday?
- How can I improve my prayer life?
- Why do churches of Christ sing without musical instruments in worship?
- What is my responsibility to the church?

Basic questions that require basic training.

By the way, basic training at Parris Island is 13 weeks long. And *Basic Training: A Manual for Teens* is also 13 weeks (or lessons) long. My hope and my prayer are that you will come out of basic training with a strong faith and a powerful commitment to Jesus Christ and His church!

CHAPTER 1

The Bible

GOD'S TRAINING MANUAL

One day a preacher visited some of his church members who wanted to impress him. Mom and Dad said to their 8-year-old daughter, "Honey, would you go into the den and get the Good Book? You know, the Book that we all love so much in this family and spend so much time reading." The little girl hurried to obey, but much to her parents' embarrassment, she came back with the *TV Guide*!

Unfortunately, for too many of us, the Bible comes in a distant second to the *TV Guide*, or some other book, when it comes to what we really value as being most important. The Bible is the dominant piece of literature in the world, with multiple billions of copies published to this point, and millions more published every year. Yet we often overlook its importance in our lives.

If you have a Bible near you right now, pick it up for a moment. Do you realize you are holding the eternal Word of Almighty God in your hand? Second Timothy 3:16-17 reads,

> All Scripture is God-breathed and is useful for teaching, rebuking, correcting and training in righteousness, so that the Man of God may be thoroughly equipped for every good work.

The Bible is literally God breathing out His message to man.

Let's take a look at two very important questions concerning the Bible.

How Is the Bible Inspired by God?

Second Timothy 3:16-17 reveals that God was actively involved in the writing of Scripture. The Bible was written by men supernaturally inspired as they were moved by the Holy Spirit, so that their writings were complete and free from error as no other writings ever have been or ever will be.

Second Peter 1:21 reads, "For prophecy never had its origin in the will of man, but men spoke from God as they were carried along by the Holy Spirit." The men who wrote Scripture did not speak of their own interpretation, but spoke and wrote as they were guided by the Holy Spirit. This means God guided the writers of Scripture so as to influence their every word.

God Used Three Methods in the Preparation and Reception of the Bible

1. Revelation. This was the process whereby the Holy Spirit spoke to the human writers of Scripture the message He wanted them to transmit. Without the Bible, we might believe in the existence of God, but we would not know who He is, what He is like, or how to get to know Him. Revelation is God filling those gaps by unveiling Himself and His will to humanity.

2. Inspiration. This process enabled the Holy Spirit to guide the pen of those 40 or so writers of Scripture so that the message would be accurately recorded.

3. Illumination. This ongoing process involves the Holy Spirit taking the written Word when it is preached, taught, read or studied and using it to enlighten us to God's truths.

What Are the Evidences That the Bible Is the Word of God?

One of the overwhelming evidences to support the Bible as the Word of God is its unparalleled unity.

• The 66 books of the Bible were written by approximately 40 different men over a period of 1600 years. Yet none of the writers –

some writing hundreds of years apart with no access to one another – contradict one another on a single issue!

- These writers came from various backgrounds, as well as different time periods and cultures. There were kings, prophets, priests, farmers and tentmakers. There were educated men, including a doctor, and uneducated fishermen, shepherds and common men. Yet they wrote as one with amazing unity.
- Many kinds of writing are used in the Bible – prophecy, psalms, proverbs, poetry, parables, personal letters, geography, history, biography, autobiography, sermons and letters, all written during times of myths, superstition and general scientific ignorance. Yet nothing written in Scripture has been proven untrue.
- The writers of the Bible used different languages and lived in several different countries, but they presented one central theme without contradiction or variation. They primarily wrote in Hebrew and Greek. In most instances the writers had no access to one another, yet they wrote one united message from God. Could that be possible short of the Bible's being what it claims to be, "God-breathed"?

Another important evidence for the Bible's being the inspired Word of God is its fulfilled prophecies and scientific foreknowledge. The Bible is the only book in the world that has specific prophecies clearly fulfilled hundreds of years after they were given. Biblical prophecies were not incidental or accidental but were God's method of proclaiming His message through the foretelling of future events. This was not *X-Files* stuff; these were definite predictions of events that would occur long after that part of the Bible was written.

These biblical prophets repeatedly made prophecies which, if not fulfilled, would prove the Bible to be untrue. Keep in mind these prophets were not like "modern-day prophets" who make a hundred predictions and maybe, by coincidence, get two or three right. Biblical prophets were always right. How was this possible? How could these prophets predict future events with 100 percent accuracy? The only logical answer is that they were given their message by the Holy Spirit, as the Bible claims in 2 Peter 1:21.

Dozens and dozens of fulfilled prophecies are mentioned in Scripture, but for the sake of space, let's just look at a few specific Old Testament prophecies concerning Jesus Christ and their fulfillment in the New Testament.

O.T. PROPHECY: Jesus would be born to a virgin. "Therefore the Lord himself will give you a sign: The virgin will be with child and will give birth to a son, and will call him Immanuel" (Isaiah 7:14).
N.T. FULFILLMENT: Jesus was born of the virgin Mary. "This is how the birth of Jesus came about. His mother Mary was pledged to be married to Joseph, but before they came together, she was found to be with child through the Holy Spirit" (Matthew 1:18).

O.T. PROPHECY: Jesus would be born in the tiny city of Bethlehem. "But you, Bethlehem Ephrathah, though you are small among the clans of Judah, out of you will come for me one who will be ruler over Israel, whose origins are from of old, from ancient times" (Micah 5:2).
N.T. FULFILLMENT: Jesus was born in an unlikely place, tiny Bethlehem. "Today in the town of David [Bethlehem] a Savior has been born to you; he is Christ the Lord" (Luke 2:11).

O.T. PROPHECY: Jesus would be abused and crucified. "But he was pierced for our transgressions, he was crushed for our iniquities; the punishment that brought us peace was upon him, and by his wounds we are healed" (Isaiah 53:5).
N.T. FULFILLMENT: Jesus was beaten and then crucified. "Then he [Pilate] released Barabbas to them. But he had Jesus flogged, and handed him over to be crucified" (Matthew 27:26).

O.T. PROPHECY: Jesus would rise from the dead. "You will not abandon me to the grave, nor will you let your Holy One see decay" (Psalm 16:10).
N.T. FULFILLMENT: Jesus rose from the dead. "The angel said to the women, 'Do not be afraid, for I know that

you are looking for Jesus, who was crucified. He is not here; he has risen just as he said. Come and see the place where he lay"' (Matthew 28:5-6).

We could continue with many more prophecies and fulfillments, and not just about Jesus, but amazingly detailed prophecies relating to time, places and people. The chance of these prophecies being accidentally fulfilled is virtually zero. These prophecies help validate the Bible's claim that it is the Word of God.

Scattered evidence in the Scriptures point to scientific foreknowledge by the writers of the Bible.

- "For the life of a creature is in the blood" (Leviticus 17:11). This fact was not proven until A.D. 1616 by William Harvey.
- In approximately 1500 B.C., Job wrote: "He suspends the earth over nothing" (26:7). This fact was not proven until A.D. 1475 by Copernicus.
- In Leviticus 13-17, a number of instructions were given about avoiding contact with a sick person. Masks and quarantines were recommended by Moses. It wasn't until the 19th century that Louis Pasteur came to many of the same conclusions about contact with the sick.
- Also in Leviticus, Moses gave the Israelites a large number of permitted and forbidden foods. Not one mistake was made in any of these nutritional commands. Given all that we have learned about nutrition in the technological age, isn't that odd? No, because God inspired the writings!

Archaeology has actually helped confirm the truth of Scripture. Many people or places that 18th and 19th century scholars questioned have now been verified as factual. Cities mentioned in the Bible but once thought to be non-existent by skeptical historians have been found. Kings once believed to be mythical characters by skeptics have been found to be historical figures as presented in the Bible.

Mistakes in the archaeological record might cause us to doubt the Bible as the Word of God. But the known facts of history agree with Scripture. In this sense, history is confirmed by the Bible, and the Bible is confirmed by history.

Another evidence pointing toward the accuracy and truth of the Bible is the fact that it has stood the test of time and proven itself to be indestructible. Many people have tried to destroy God's Word, but they have failed because the Word of God will stand forever:

> The grass withers and the flowers fall, but the word of our God stands forever (Isaiah 40:8).

> For you have been born again, not of perishable seed, but of imperishable, through the living and enduring word of God. For, "All men are like grass, and all their glory is like the flowers of the field; the grass withers and the flowers fall, but the word of the Lord stands forever" (1 Peter 1:23-25).

Atheism has not made a dent in the indestructibility of the Bible; neither has humanism, rationalism, liberalism, philosophy or any political movement. Over the course of history when the Bible has been attacked, its attackers fell, and Scripture stands just as promised. Even if, by some insidious plan of Satan, every copy of the Bible could be destroyed, you could get a group of Christians together and write every word of it again because it dwells within the hearts of God's people all over the world. Its indestructibility in the face of many opponents testifies to its truth and accuracy.

Finally, the transforming power of changed lives testify to the truth of the Bible. Good self-help books come and go within the span of a generation or so, but not the Book! No other writing has had the transforming and life-changing power of the Bible.

The hearts and lives of multiplied millions of people have been dramatically changed as a result of their becoming Christians and following the truths of the Bible. Count me among those people. Can we, should we, ignore such relational evidence concerning the truth and accuracy of the Bible?

Not one of these evidences, standing alone, proves that the Bible is the Word of God. but taken together they produce overwhelming evidence to support the belief that the Bible is exactly what it claims to be – the divinely inspired, error-free, perfect Word of God!

As the old children's song goes:
> The B-I-B-L-E
> Yes, that's the book for me.
> I'll stand upon the Word of God.
> The B-I-B-L-E!

Talking Back

1. Did you believe the Bible was the Word of God before reading this chapter? If so, why? Does this chapter add to your confidence? If so, in what ways?

2. Which evidence listed to support the Bible as the Word of God is most convincing to you?

3. How did fallible men write and record an infallible Bible? How can we then understand the Bible's message?

4. What influence has the Bible had on society?

5. Why do you think people often tend to forget or ignore the Bible's message?

Exercising Your Faith

Get a copy of the *One-Year Bible* and commit to reading the Bible through in a year. You'll see the difference it will make in your life!

ALMIGHTY INTELLIGENCE

CHAPTER 2

God, the Father

COMMANDER-IN-CHIEF

I spent much of my childhood and early adolescence terrified of Steve Jennette. Steve was two years older and much bigger than I was and was recognized locally as the neighborhood bully. Rumor had it he regularly beat up other kids up just for fun. The irony was that none of us ever were personally beat up by him, but we heard he could do it and had done it, and that was enough to convince us.

The funny thing was, the few times I ran into him personally, he seemed like an okay guy. It is distinctly possible Steve was not nearly the villain we made him out to be in our minds. But perception is often reality, and our perceptions scared us.

It seems to me that God has also picked up an undeserved bad reputation in the minds of many people. He is often thought of as a vengeful judge or a stern taskmaster.

A little boy named Johnny was having a dispute with his mother about green beans. Johnny's mother was trying her best to persuade the boy to eat his green beans, but he wouldn't budge. Finally, in desperation, she said, "Johnny, if you don't eat your green beans, God will punish you!" Still Johnny refused, and his mother sent him to bed.

A short time later, a tremendous storm arose. Lightning flashed, great thunder shook the house, and torrents of rain fell. Johnny's mother rushed upstairs to check on her son.

"Johnny, are you okay?" she asked.

"I guess so," he replied. "But this sure is an awful fuss to make about a few green beans."

A little girl was once asked, "What do you think God is like?"

"The sort of person who is always snooping around to see if anyone is having a good time and trying to stop it," she replied.

Of course, most people would not admit that God is sort of a heavenly killjoy. In fact, openly they would speak about His love and call Him "Father." But beneath the words you may hear the truth: Many people feel about God the way I felt about Steve Jennette!

Word Association

What is the first thing that comes to your mind when you hear the word "God"?

J.B. Phillips in *Your God Is Too Small* identified images many people have of God:

- **Resident Policeman.** This image pictures God as a traffic cop seeking to catch us speeding and giving us a ticket for the maximum fine.
- **Grand Old Man.** To some people, God is a grandfatherly gentleman with a long beard and gray hair who sits on a great throne up there somewhere peering down at His world.
- **Parental Hangover.** Some psychologists propose that our early concept of God is closely related to our idea of an earthly father. Therefore, if our father was kind and loving, so is our image of God. If our father was distant and abusive, so is our image of God.
- **Managing Director.** This view of God makes Him a magnified human being, responsible for the successful operation of a vast universe. He could not possibly be expected to take interest in our individual lives since He is so busy managing the whole world.

These are but a few of the common images people have of God, the Father. When we played the word association game a moment ago, did any of these pictures come to your mind?

Our goal in this chapter will be to determine a true definition of God. We cannot invent a definition of God and expect it to be true. He is much more than a resident policeman, a managing director or a kindly grandfather.

Will the Real God Please Stand Up?

We get a proper understanding of the nature and characteristics of God from the Bible. Let's look at how the Bible defines God:

God is eternal. God always was and always will be. He is "from everlasting to everlasting" (Psalm 90:1-2). This should be a comforting thought and make us feel secure. God always has been and always will be, and we are His significant and loved children.

God is omnipresent. Don't be scared away by that big word. It simply means God is everywhere simultaneously (Psalm 139:7-12). Both a blessing and a warning are in this truth. The blessing is that God is always with the Christian and will never forsake him. On the other hand, it can be chilling to realize that God sees all we do, hears all we say, and even knows all we think.

God is omnipotent. The word "omni" means all, and the word "potent" means powerful; thus, God is all-powerful. It took an all-powerful God to create the universe and to sustain it. Job 42:2 reads, "I know that you can do all things; no plan of yours can be thwarted."

God is omniscient. This means He is all-knowing. Psalm 147:5 says, "Great is our Lord and mighty in power; his understanding has no limit." There is no fooling God. The prophet Jeremiah wrote, "I the Lord search the heart and examine the mind, to reward a man according to his conduct, according to what his deeds deserve" (Jeremiah 17:10).

God is unchanging. Malachi 3:6 records, "I the Lord do not change." James 1:17 says that God "does not change like shifting shadows." Friends may change, families may change, but God never changes. He is always consistent, constant, reliable and dependable. He is the same yesterday, today and forever (Hebrews 13:8).

God is holy. God has never sinned; He is incapable of sin because His very nature is to be holy, set apart from sin. It is not that He has the ability to live up to some model of holiness; He is the model. "Holy, holy, holy is the Lord Almighty; the whole earth is full of his glory" (Isaiah 6:3).

God is merciful. Ephesians 2:4 says that God is "rich in mercy." We deserve to die because of our sins, but a merciful God sent His Son to die for our sins. Aren't you glad God is merciful? Aren't you glad he gave us what we need, not what we deserve? That's mercy!

God is light. "God is light: in him there is no darkness at all" (1 John 1:5). People speak a universal language that says we love light and fear darkness. Light stands for truth, justice and holiness. Darkness stands for sin, injustice and death. It is little wonder that John described God as "light." The Lord will be your light when you fear the darkness. He will be for you what He was for King David: "The Lord is my light and my salvation – whom shall I fear?" (Psalm 27:1).

God is loving and intimate. In Romans 8:15, the word "Abba" is used for God. It is our more intimate word "daddy" or "papa." So, yes, God is our great omnipotent, omnipresent and omniscient God, but He is also our Papa, our personal Father! Undoubtedly, many people find Christianity boring, ritualistic, cold and impersonal because they do not have the proper concept of God. They only have His greatness concept and have not recognized that He is also a personal, intimate Father God. His intimacy toward you is a reflection of His love for you. How much does He love You?

> For God so loved the world that he gave his one and only Son, that whoever believes in him shall not perish but have eternal life (John 3:16).

Perhaps the two deepest desires of the human heart are the desires for love and purpose. These are desires God has given us because He wants to be the one to fulfill them. In fact, He is the only One who can satisfy them fully. He loves us as His creation and His children, and He provides us with life's greatest purpose – to love, serve and obey Him in return.

His Word says, "If you love me, you will keep what I command" (John 14:15). Keeping His commandments is for our own good. He created us and loves us and knows what is best for us.
- When He asks you to be sexually pure, it is for your own good. It is harmful to you when you are not.
- When He tells you to "honor your father and your mother" and "obey your parents" (Ephesians 6:1-2), it is for your own good.

It is harmful to you when you don't.

- When He says to be careful about dating a non-Christian (2 Corinthians 6:14-17), it is for your own good. Don't you trust God to take care of your relationship needs?
- When He asks you to be honest and act with integrity, it is for your own good. It is harmful to you when you are not.
- When He tells you to forgive unconditionally, it is for your own good. He knows that unforgiveness is a bitter root, a cancer, that grows in your heart and soul.

Many reasons exist to love and obey God: respect for Him, to return His love and blessings, thankfulness, to give a good testimony to others. But in addition to all these good reasons to obey God, a primary reason is because it is best for you.

When you are tempted to disobey God, the Father, remind yourself who He is. Remind yourself how much He loves you. Remind yourself how He wants the best for you. And then love, trust and obey Him. You are the one who will suffer if you don't. And you are the one who will be blessed if you do.

One very important question remains: What is your relationship to God, the Father? If it is less than what it should be, give yourself to Him completely – today.

Talking Back

1. Play the word association game. What first comes to your mind when you hear the word "God"?

2. Of the common images of God listed in this chapter, which one would you most likely have? Which one do you think most people have? Why?

3. Which characteristic of God seems most wonderful to you? Are any of them a bit troubling to you?

4. Do you think keeping God's commandments is for your own good?

5. If you could ask God any question, what would it be?

Exercising Your Faith

Write God a letter saying anything you want to say, asking any question you want to ask, making requests, etc. Keep the letter and look back at it in a month or two. Make it an every month practice, a sort of "God Journal."

Ask a sampling of people who don't attend church with you – classmates, teachers, co-workers, etc. – who Jesus is. Be prepared to share your findings next week.

CHAPTER 3

Jesus, the Savior

RESCUE
MISSION

If you were to ask 10 people around the world at random who Jesus is, you might get 10 different answers:

1. A man, just like any other human being,
2. A great moral teacher,
3. An historical figure in Jewish history.
4. The founder of one of the world's great religions,
5. A madman,
6. A mythical character in a book,
7. An instigator of evil, such as the Crusades, religious wars, animal sacrifices,
8. Never heard of Him.
9. A name to curse and swear by.
10. The Savior.

If you had to describe Jesus Christ to someone who had never heard of Him, what would you say?

To merely say He was a great man or a great moral teacher is not enough. He claimed to be God. He said He could forgive sins. He repeated one outrageous thing after another which, if not true, would prevent us from saying He was a great moral teacher.

He was born of a virgin, ministered God's will on earth, died for our sins, was resurrected, ascended into heaven, and will come again someday to usher in the Judgment Day. He is the Son of God.

Near the end of 1999, a group of theologians voted on the Top 100 religious books of the 20th century. Their choice for No. 1 was *Mere Christianity* by C.S. Lewis. Here's what Lewis had to say on the subject of Jesus being merely a great moral teacher:

I am trying here to prevent anyone saying the really fool-
ish thing that people often say about Jesus: "I'm ready to
accept Jesus as a great moral teacher, but I don't accept
His claim to be God." That is the one thing we must not
say. A man who said the sorts of things Jesus said would
not be a great moral teacher. He would either be a lunatic
– on the level of a man who says he is a poached egg – or
else he would be the devil of hell. You must make your
choice. Either this man was, and is, the Son of God, or else
a madman or something worse. You can shut him up for a
fool, you can spit at him and kill him as a demon, or you
can fall at his feet and call him Lord and God. But let us
not come with any patronizing nonsense about his being
a great human teacher. He has not left that open to us. He
did not intend to.

Author Josh McDowell expounds on Lewis' words in *Evidence
That Demands a Verdict*:

He was either a liar, or a lunatic, or the Lord. He said He
was the Son of God, that He knew the future, that He was
without sin, that He could forgive sins, and that people
would go to heaven if they believed in Him and received
Him as their personal Savior. If those things aren't true,
and He knew they weren't, He was a liar. If those things
weren't true, but He thought they were, He was a lunatic.
Or, if those things were true, He is the Lord.

Indeed, Jesus is Lord!

Why Do We Need Jesus Christ?

God made human beings in His own image (Genesis 1:26). He
took a calculated risk when He made people free because they
could choose to deny or disobey Him. God desired to love and be
loved. But He made us with free will and choice because He wanted our love to be free and spontaneous.

When mankind chose the route of sin and rebellion, the result
was separation from God. This separation broke the heart of God

who created us to be in fellowship with Him.

God was faced with a challenging problem. How could a holy God and sinful people be brought together? He could not condemn all humanity because that would be inconsistent with His love. Yet He could not save humanity indiscriminately because that would be inconsistent with His justice.

God chose to send a mediator who would pay the price He Himself demanded, leaving the decision with people of free will. That mediator was His Son, Jesus. You have probably heard the word "incarnation" to describe the birth of Christ. The word simply means "in the flesh." In the incarnation we are confronted with a great miracle – God revealed Himself in a flesh and blood body:

> The Word became flesh and made his dwelling among us (John 1:14).

> For in Christ all the fullness of the Deity lives in bodily form (Colossians 2:9).

No human could ever pay the price for another's sins because the one who would volunteer to pay the price for another would himself deserve to die. The only one who could pay the price for us was someone who was sinless and did not deserve to die. And the only person who ever fit that description is Jesus. That is why we need Jesus Christ.

What Was Jesus Like?

Jesus was born into a human family. It is difficult to imagine God as a fetus and then a tiny infant, but those emphasize His humanity. Although He was fully divine, He was also fully human. He experienced the same temptations we encounter:

> For we do not have a high priest who is unable to sympathize with our weaknesses, but we have one who has been tempted in every way, just as we are – yet was without sin (Hebrews 4:15).

Jesus was compassionate. He healed the sick, gave sight to the blind, hearing to the deaf, and life to the dead. He fed the hungry, cast out demons, and gave living water to the thirsty. Jesus didn't perform these miracles merely to impress or entertain. He helped people out of a sense of compassion. He helped people because He loved them.

Jesus had an appealing personality. He attracted huge crowds, but He also had time for the individual. He crossed all social, economic and political barriers, as people with great charisma often do. He attracted kings, common people, religious leaders, political leaders, prostitutes, hated tax collectors and small children alike. There was just something about Jesus that appealed to everyone.

Jesus was a man of action. There was no "Do as I say, not as I do" attitude in Jesus. He practiced what He preached. He acted as no other man ever acted. He overthrew the money-changing religious frauds in the temple (John 2:13-16). He raised a man from the dead after four days in the grave (John 11:17-44). He healed a demon-possessed man (Luke 8:26-35). He gave sight to a blind man (Mark 10:46-52). He rescued a sinful woman from her hypocritical prosecutors (John 8:1-11). He healed 10 lepers, although only one expressed gratitude (Luke 17:11-19). Jesus didn't just talk about doing good – His motto was "Just Do It."

Jesus was perfect and sinless. Although He was "tempted in every way just as we are," He was "yet without sin" (Hebrews 4:15). It required a sinless One to be sacrificed for sinful ones like you and me. Jesus was that sinless sacrifice: "God made him who had no sin to be sin for us, so that in him we might become the righteousness of God" (2 Corinthians 5:21).

What Is Jesus' Primary Ministry?

Jesus' primary ministry is to serve as the mediator between God and man:

> For there is one God and one mediator between God and men, the man Christ Jesus, who gave himself as a ransom for all men (1 Timothy 2:5-6).

A mediator is a middleman, one who comes between two parties to reconcile their differences. Our sin separates us from God, and death is the penalty for sin (Romans 5:12). So a mediator was necessary to resolve the differences between sinful mankind and a holy God, between sin and justice. Jesus Christ is the only mediator.

Keep in mind that a mediator must consider the interests of both parties. In this instance, our Mediator, Jesus, does not want us to pay for our sins with eternal death, but He also must consider the interests of a righteous, just and holy God. On God's side, justice must be satisfied, while on man's side, the sinner must be justified. On the cross of Calvary, Jesus, the Mediator, paid the price for sin and all at once satisfied the justice of God and justified sinners who trust and obey Him.

As our mediator, Jesus succeeded by making peace between us and God, changing us from God's enemies to God's children:

> For God was pleased to have all his fullness dwell in him, and through him to reconcile to himself all things, whether things on earth or things in heaven, by making peace through his blood, shed on the cross. Once you were alienated from God and were enemies in your minds because of your evil behavior. But now he has reconciled you by Christ's physical body through death to present you holy in his sight, without blemish and free from accusation (Colossians 1:19-22).

What a Mediator! What a Savior!

No words exist to describe adequately the character, ministry and love of Jesus Christ, but an unknown author years ago came close by writing an essay that has circulated around the world:

> He was born in an obscure village, the child of a peasant woman. He grew up in another obscure village where He worked in a carpenter shop until He was 30. Then for three years He was an itinerant [traveling] preacher.
>
> He never had a family or owned a home. He never set foot inside a big city. He never traveled 200 miles from the place He was born. He never wrote a book or held an office. He did none of the things that usually accompany greatness.

While He was still a young man, the tide of popular opinion turned against Him. His friends deserted Him. He was turned over to His enemies, and went through the mockery of a trial. He was nailed to a cross between two thieves. While He was dying, His executioners gambled for the only piece of property He had – His coat.

When He was dead, He was taken down and laid in a borrowed grave. [Twenty] centuries have come and gone, and today He is the central figure for much of the human race. All the armies that ever marched and all the navies that ever sailed and all the parliaments that ever sat and all the kings that ever reigned put together have not affected the life of man upon this earth as powerfully as this

ONE SOLITARY LIFE.

Talking Back

1. If you had to describe Jesus Christ to someone who had never heard of Him, what would you say?
2. Why was Jesus either a liar, a lunatic or the Lord?
3. Of the characteristics of Jesus listed in the chapter, which is most appealing to you and why?
4. How would you describe Jesus' ministry and mission?
5. Why do you think some people reject Jesus?

Exercising Your Faith

What were some of the answers you received last week when you asked "Who is Jesus?"

Go to the library and check out either C.S. Lewis' *Mere Christianity* or Josh McDowell's *Evidence That Demands a Verdict*. Study Jesus for yourself so that your faith is real and personal, not merely inherited.

CHAPTER 4

The Holy Spirit
IN THE
TRENCHES

When I was growing up, the Holy Spirit was almost always referred to as the Holy Ghost, which is the title used in the King James Version of the Bible. As a kid I thought it sounded spooky. The only ghost I was familiar with was the cartoon character, Casper the Friendly Ghost, so it was a confusing term to me.

During my teen years I remember thinking, "God is my Father, and Jesus is His Son. I can understand that and relate to them. But what is the Holy Ghost?" So I decided to settle for two out of three until years later.

Don't let that happen to you. Put on your thinking cap. Although the concept is difficult to understand, we must talk about the Trinity – the doctrine of the union of three persons (Father, Son and Holy Spirit) in one Godhead.

Attempts to understand fully the doctrine of the Trinity fall short, as do all attempts to explain God fully. Yet the New Testament clearly presents one God who relates to human beings in three persons.

How do we explain the mystery of the Trinity? We don't, but illustrations may help. The word "God" is a family name, not just a personal name. It doesn't refer to just one person, but to a family – the Father, the Son and the Holy Spirit. Think of three individuals with the same family name, God.

When the Bible says there is one God, the oneness is not the numeral as in 1, 2, 3, but it is the unity of one nest, or one family. It is the same principle as in Matthew 19:5-6, referring to marriage, where Jesus said, "the two shall become one flesh." They do not become numerically one, but in unity one, experiencing "oneness." The Father, the Son and the Holy Spirit are separate persons with distinct personalities and works, but they are in unity and oneness a single Deity.

I have found it helpful to compare the Trinity to a drama. Let's think of the Bible as a drama being acted out on a stage. In the Old Testament, the Father is in the center of the stage, while the Son and the Spirit are on either side. In the New Testament gospels, the Son is in the center of the stage, while the Father and the Spirit are on either side. Beginning with Acts, the Spirit is in center stage, while the Father and Son are on either side. Yet, at all times and in every situation, Father, Son and Spirit are present and involved in both the plot and the action.

The Characteristics of the Holy Spirit

The Holy Spirit is a real person. It is tempting to see God as a He (the Father), as a He (the Son), and as an It (the Holy Spirit). But the Bible describes the Holy Spirit as having a personality, the characteristics of a person.

He loves. "I urge you, brothers, by our Lord Jesus Christ and by the love of the Spirit, to join me in my struggle by praying to God for me" (Romans 15:30).

He has a will. "All these are the work of one and the same Spirit, and He gives them to each one, just as he determines" (1 Corinthians 12:11).

He has emotions, such as grief. "And do not grieve the Holy Spirit of God, with whom you were sealed for the day of redemption" (Ephesians 4:30).

He prays.

> In the same way, the Spirit helps us in our weakness. We do not know what we ought to pray, but the Spirit himself intercedes for us with groans that words cannot express. And he who searches our hearts knows the mind of the Spirit, because the Spirit intercedes for the saints in accordance with God's will (Romans 8:26-27).

He teaches. "This is what we speak, not in words taught us by human wisdom but in words taught by the Spirit, expressing spiritual truths in spiritual words" (1 Corinthians 2:13).

The Holy Spirit is also God. He not only has characteristics of a real person, but He also has characteristics only God has.

He helped create the world. "Now the earth was formless and empty, darkness was over the surface of the deep, and the Spirit of God was hovering over the waters" (Genesis 1:2).

He helped create mankind. "Then God said, 'Let us make man in our image, in our likeness'" (Genesis 1:26). Who is "us"? God, the Father, the Son and the Holy Spirit.

He is eternal.

> How much more, then, will the blood of Christ, who through the eternal Spirit offered himself unblemished to God, cleanse our consciences from acts that lead to death, so that we may serve the living God! (Hebrews 9:14).

What Is the Holy Spirit's Primary Ministry?

A constant tug-of-war goes on between our sinful desires (the flesh) and the Spirit (Romans 8:5-17; Galatians 5:16-27). The Holy Spirit's primary ministry is to help us defeat the sinful desires within us. He accomplishes this in three ways:

1. The Spirit helps us to be spiritually minded.

> Those who live according to the sinful nature have their minds set on what that nature desires; but those who live in accordance with the Spirit have their minds set on what the Spirit desires. The mind of sinful man is death, but the mind controlled by the Spirit is life and peace (Romans 8:5-6).

Sin always begins as a seed in the mind, the thought processes. It is a work of the Holy Spirit to help us control our mind and thoughts.

2. The Spirit helps us to win over sin. Romans 8:13 reads: "For if you live according to the sinful nature, you will die; but if by the Spirit you put to death the misdeeds of the body, you will live." It is the Holy Spirit who enables us to battle the desires of the flesh

and obtain the strength to overcome temptation. In this way, the Spirit helps us win over sin.

3. The Spirit helps us in our weaknesses. "In the same way, the Spirit helps us in our weakness" (Romans 8:26). Human nature is naturally weak. Only the Spirit of God can make us strong enough to overcome the enemy, Satan.

How Do We Respond to the Holy Spirit?

The New Testament describes three ways we can respond to the ministry of the Holy Spirit. In fact, if you are a Christian, the Holy Spirit is working in your life this very minute. You may not be aware of it, but He is.

Learning to recognize the Holy Spirit is the first step in learning to live the Spirit-filled life. Galatians 5:18 says that we should be led by the Spirit. If we are to be led by the Spirit, it would certainly help if we could recognize Him.

Let's take a look at the three ways we respond to the Holy Spirit:

1. We are to be filled with the Spirit. Ephesians 5:18 reads: "Do not get drunk on wine which leads to debauchery. Instead, be filled with the Spirit." What does that mean?

These Ephesian Christians had already received the gift of the indwelling Holy Spirit at baptism (Acts 2:38), as all believers do. So what is the difference between the indwelling of the Spirit and being filled with the Spirit? Think of it in terms of this illustration:

A guest is invited into your home. But upon entering your home, he is immediately confined to a small room somewhere near the front door. For a while you may even forget he is there. Finally, you realize this is no way to treat a guest, so you give him free access to every room in your home.

In this illustration, the Holy Spirit is, of course, your invited guest. You are the Christian, and the house stands for your life. The difference then between the indwelling of the Spirit and the filling of the Spirit is the difference between being confined in a small room and being given free access to all the rooms.

The filling of the Spirit does not mean the Christian gets more of the Spirit, but rather the Spirit gets more of the Christian.

2. We should not neglect the Holy Spirit. "Do not put out the Spirit's fire" (1 Thessalonians 5:19). The King James Version says, "Quench not the Spirit." This involves not doing what the Holy Spirit would have us do. Some have called this a "sin of omission," neglecting to do what the Bible tells us to do and what the Spirit would have us do.

3. We should not grieve the Holy Spirit. "And do not grieve the Holy Spirit of God with whom you were sealed for the day of redemption" (Ephesians 4:30). This involves doing what the Holy Spirit would not have us do. Some have called this a "sin of commission," willingly and knowingly committing sins we know displease God and grieve the Holy Spirit. Think of it in terms of this illustration:

You board an airplane today bound for my hometown, Ft. Myers, Fla., to visit. You find yourself sitting next to an unbeliever and have several opportunities to share Christ with him, but you remain silent. You even think that you should tell him you are a Christian, but you never do. At this point, you may have put out the Spirit's fire by not doing what the Spirit wanted you to do.

As the flight continues, you introduce yourselves and begin talking, but not about spiritual matters. In fact, to your shame, several off-color stories and jokes are exchanged. At this point, you may have grieved the Holy Spirit by doing what the Spirit did not want you to do.

My purpose in this chapter has been to explore the doctrine of the Holy spirit. My hope is that the Spirit will be more real and, therefore, more believable to you now. And my desire is that you will seek to be filled with the Spirit and avoid neglecting or grieving the Holy Spirit of God!

Talking Back

1. When you hear the terms "Holy Spirit" or "Holy Ghost," what images or thoughts come to your mind?

2. What was your understanding of the Trinity before reading this chapter? Has your understanding of the Trinity changed?

3. What ministry of the Holy Spirit means the most to you?

4. What seems like the most important characteristic of the Holy Spirit to you?

5. Answer in your own words these three questions:

   a. What does it mean to be filled with the Spirit?

   b. What does it mean not to put out the Spirit's fire?

   c. What does it mean not to grieve the Spirit?

Exercising Your Faith

Read 1 Corinthians 12:4-11; Ephesians 4:11-12; Romans 12:4-8; and 1 Peter 4:10. What gift(s) do you think the Holy Spirit may have given you? What would you like to do with it?

CHAPTER 5

What Is Faith?
UNKNOWN
TERRITORY

aith is the very essence of Christianity. And faith, if it is to be effective, must be intensely personal not merely inherited.

Perhaps you have heard about the man who fell over the side of a cliff and grabbed a small tree just before plummeting hundreds of feet to his death. As he hung there, he cried out desperately for someone to help him and a deep, booming voice came from all around him.

"Do you trust Me?"

"Who are you?" the man asked.

The Voice replied, "This is the Lord. Do you trust Me?"

The man said, "Yes, Lord, yes! I'm glad it's You. I trust You. Help me!"

"All right, let go of the branch, and I'll save you," the Voice said.

"Wha-a-a-t did You say, Lord?" the man gasped.

"Let go of the branch," was the reply.

The man was silent for several moments. Then he cried out, "Is there anyone else up there?"

Many Christians are like the man holding onto the small tree. They say they believe in God, believe in Christ, and believe in the church, but when the Lord calls for them to turn loose of the "small tree of this world" that cannot save them, they want to know if there is someone else up there – someone who won't call on them to live by faith, not by sight (2 Corinthians 5:7).

We usually act on what we really believe. So, if God tells us to let go or hang on, we obey if we trust Him. But if we doubt, we do whatever we think will be best for us. This chapter is designed to define faith, increase it, and move it from mere belief to action in our lives.

What Faith Is

The Bible says, "Now faith is being sure of what we hope for and certain of what we do not see" (Hebrews 11:1). Another translation says, "Now faith means putting our full confidence in the things we hope for; it means being certain of things we cannot see." So, faith is an inner confidence and trust in something or someone beyond the realm of human knowledge or understanding.

We live in such a visual society. Perhaps that is why so many people have a problem with faith. "I'll have to see it to believe it" is a common motto. But the truth is, we are not consistent with that practice. There are many things we have faith in that we may not see or fully understand. The great inventor Thomas Edison said,

> We don't know the millionth part of one percent about anything. We don't know what water is. We don't know what light is. We don't know what gravitation is. We don't know what heat is. We have a lot of hypotheses about these things but that is all.

In a similar sense, we may not understand everything about God (the Bible admits there are mysteries, 1 Corinthians 2:7-11), but we can still have faith.

What Faith Is Not

Faith is not just believing. Faith's value lies not in the believing, but in what you believe. You can believe anything. If what you believe is true, you benefit; if what you believe is not true, you lose. In both cases, believing is the same, only the objects of that belief vary. As important as belief is, it is insufficient alone, for James 2:19 says, "Even the demons believe – and shudder."

Faith is not just believing in a set of principles. Faith isn't like trigonometry where you believe a table of logarithms is correct. You never use them, so you never have reason to doubt them.

Faith isn't just an opinion about life. Faith is a way of life. It is the door that lets God into one's life.

Faith is not fantasy or wishful thinking. Faith doesn't disregard reality; it embraces it. Attitudes always reflect themselves in actions.

Faith is not a means of coercing God. Often we want things and think that if only we had faith, God would give them to us. But God may know that what we want isn't best for us at that time. Faith is not a way of trying to manipulate God into giving us what we want.

What Does Faith Do for Us?

First, faith can give you confidence for living. Faith will help you stand up to the pressures, tensions and stresses of life. It will give you a sense of victory and assurance, helping you to be hopeful and confident. You can have this confidence as you realize you are "more than conquerors through him who loved us" (Romans 8:37).

Second, faith can make you more loving. Love is the single most important characteristic of the Christian faith (1 Corinthians 13:13) and probably the best test of your spiritual temperature. Jesus said,

> A new command I give you: Love one another. As I have loved you, so you must love one another. By this all men will know that you are my disciples if you love one another (John 13:34-35).

Are you more loving now than you were, say, at this time last year? Are you more loving toward your family? Your friends? Your Lord? Growing in faith will make you more loving.

Psychologist Robert Minneair said,

> If you really want to be happy, then pretend for one month that every person you meet is the most important person in the world, that is, relate to everybody you see as if he or she is the most important person in the world.

That's a good idea, but the Christian faith calls us to an even higher standard – it tells us to treat every person we meet as if he or she were Jesus Himself (Matthew 25:31-46). As you follow Jesus' way, your faith will make you more loving.

Third, faith can help you in practical daily living. To be any good at all, our faith must work in the workaday world. As it grows and settles in our heart, faith keeps us from cheating at school or yelling at bad drivers or being hostile toward family and friends. Faith, if it is to be effective, must work for us every day, not just Sunday!

Fourth, faith can give you a sense of partnership with God. Living by faith will help you go into every day saying, "I am a child of God. The Lord is working on me and in me. God is with me. I am His workmanship (cf. Ephesians 2:10), and He is working through me!"

If you will take up that attitude of faith and that spirit of partnership with God, your life will be changed incredibly for the better, and you will see that faith makes a wonderful difference in your life.

Practical Guidelines for Understanding Faith

Realize that faith is a common occurrence. Faith is not a phenomenon reserved just for emotional people who can't make it in life without a crutch. Faith is an experience of every person. The question we all face is not, "Do we have faith or not?" but "In what and to what extent do we have faith?" Everyone must believe or have faith in something and to some degree.

Start with the faith you have and go from there. Don't worry that you do not seem to have the faith of others. Start with the faith you do have and use it. Pray that God will increase your faith (Luke 17:5). Invest it. Act upon it. It will grow.

Don't allow your faith to fluctuate because of moods or feelings. In his classic book *Mere Christianity*, C.S. Lewis defined faith as "the art of holding on to things your reason has once accepted, in spite of your changing moods." In the New Testament, the word "faith" appears 234 times and the word "believe" 251 times. Yet the word "feel" appears only five times and even then not in the context of telling us how to live. Make faith rule over your emotions and feelings, and not vice versa!

Feed your faith. It will not automatically remain strong; it must be fed. How do you feed faith? By regular Bible study, a consistent prayer life, meaningful worship, fellowship with other Christians, and service to others. Faith that is not regularly fed will be malnourished and eventually die.

Choose your thoughts carefully. Philippians 4:8 reads, "Finally, brothers, whatever is true, whatever is noble, whatever is right, whatever is pure, whatever is lovely, whatever is admirable – if anything is excellent or praiseworthy – think about such things." Our faith is greatly influenced by our thought processes. The person who thinks he is beaten is beaten before he even starts. Why think negative, destructive, harmful thoughts when you can think positive, uplifting ones? Choose thoughts that build you up instead of tearing you down. Choose thoughts that encourage and cultivate faith.

Be patient with your faith. There are no spiritual shortcuts to great faith. Give God time to work a quality product in you.

Understand the three-part definition of faith.

1. Faith is knowledgeable. You must know something before you can believe it. This is why faith is so closely linked to studying the Word of God: "Consequently, faith comes from hearing the message, and the message is heard through the word of Christ" (Romans 10:17).

2. Faith is mental assent or agreement. This is believing what you know. Without this assent, you have unbelief. However, faith must not stop with mere mental assent – it must move on to action.

3. Faith is action. James wrote that faith without deeds, or action, is dead (James 2:14-26). Faith is an active trust that leads to obedience (Romans 10:13-17).

These three elements – knowledge, mental assent and action – produce faith in the heart. Faith is not fulfilled if any are missing. Without knowledge, faith is over-emotional, perhaps even irrational. Without mental assent, there is unbelief. Without action, faith is dead.

Consider this story. A man had gotten so caught up in the hectic pace of everyday life that he had become almost like a zombie. He was just going through the motions, working long and hard hours and then coming home, tired, discouraged and irritable.

There was no joy, no fun, no laughter, no zest for life left in him. His wife and 4-year-old daughter noticed it, of course, but they didn't know what to do. He would come home and just sit silently, only occasionally speaking to them and then snapping at them.

One night, the man was reading the newspaper on the couch in the den, using the paper to shut out the rest of the family. Suddenly, his 4-year-old daughter pushed the newspaper down, jumped into his lap, put her little arms around his neck, and hugged him tightly. Flustered, the father said to her, "Wait a minute, honey. You are hugging me to death!"

"Oh, no, Daddy," she cried out. "I'm hugging you to life!"

That's what God does for us in faith. He hugs us to life. Live a life of faith!

Talking Back

1. In your own words, how would you define faith?
2. Why is faith so hard for so many people?
3. Reflecting on the four things listed that faith does for us, which is most meaningful to you and why?
4. How does faith differ from feelings? Why is it dangerous to allow our faith to follow our feelings?
5. How do you think a person can best feed or grow his or her faith?

Exercising Your Faith

Since faith is action, put your faith into action. This week find some act of service and faith to perform for someone else in the name of the Lord. Examples: Visit a nursing home, send a card to a sick person, volunteer to babysit free for a young couple, work in a soup kitchen, etc. The important thing is to *do* something to express your faith!

CHAPTER 6

What Is Repentance?

RETREAT!

Perhaps you have heard of the Nobel Peace Prize. What you may not know is the story of how the Nobel Peace Prize originated. In a sense, it is a story of repentance or change.

One morning in 1888, Alfred Nobel, the inventor of dynamite, awoke to find his own obituary in the newspaper. It was printed by mistake; Nobel's brother was the one who had died, and the reporter carelessly reported the wrong death.

Nobel was shocked not only to see his own obituary but also to see himself as the world saw him. He was portrayed as the Dynamite King, a man who had made an immense fortune from creating explosives and weapons of war. He was pictured as simply a merchant of death, and that morning he saw how he would be remembered.

Nobel vowed that morning that he would spend the remainder of his life changing that image and working for peace. His last will and testament left his vast fortune to honor those who have benefited mankind. One of those recognitions is the Nobel Peace Prize.

Nobel experienced a change of heart and direction; that is really the definition of repentance. The word "repentance" literally means a change of mind, will and direction.

Genuine repentance can be painful. It hurts our pride and wounds our ego. But it is a necessary hurt. Repentance has been described this way: "It hurts so much I want to quit it."

God commands our repentance. It's not an optional matter. God wants so much for us to repent and to change our heart and direction when we sin. Then He can show Himself to us as a gracious God ready to forgive, slow to anger and full of mercy.

What Repentance Is Not

Repentance is not just remorse or sorrow. Second Corinthians 7:9-10 reads:

> Yet now I am happy, not because you were made sorry, but because your sorrow led you to repentance. For you became sorrowful as God intended and so were not harmed in any way by us. Godly sorrow brings repentance that leads to salvation, and leaves no regret, but worldly sorrow brings death.

This Scripture clearly teaches that there are two kinds of sorrow: godly and worldly. What is the difference between the two?

Worldly sorrow is self-centered remorse over the painful consequences of sin. This is the type of sorrow experienced by many people in prisons and jails. They are not sorry for their wrongdoing, lawbreaking or sin but are simply sorry they were caught and are having to suffer the consequences.

Godly sorrow has two defining characteristics that distinguish it from worldly sorrow:

1. It leads to repentance, a change of mind, will and direction (v. 9).

2. It leaves no regret about being caught. True godly sorrow would be glad about being caught because it leads to repentance and freedom from sin, guilt and regret.

Repentance is not just conviction about sin. Certainly everyone of us needs to be convicted about our own sinfulness. We must recognize that we are eternally lost in our sin without Jesus Christ. But a person can be convicted about his or her sin and still not repent. In the Old Testament, King Saul said, "I have sinned" several times (1 Samuel 15:24, 30; 26:21), but he didn't genuinely repent. He would go right back immediately to the same sinful actions. So, conviction about our sins can lead to true repentance, but it is not repentance.

Repentance is not just fear. There are two kinds of fear – godly fear (respect) and simply being scared. In Ecclesiastes 12:13, Solomon said that to fear God and keep His commandments is the whole duty of man. The person who has no fear of God has reached the most dangerous position one can occupy. A Christian should fear God in the sense that he reverences and respects God, but a person can simply be scared of God and not repent. James 2:19 says that even the demons shudder about God, but they didn't repent. So, repentance is not simply fear.

Repentance is not just reform. One can reform his life without ever truly repenting. Many people reform to get off drugs or alcohol, to help their family situation, to improve their image or to convince others they have turned over a new leaf and made a fresh start. But God doesn't want reform cases; He wants new creations (2 Corinthians 5:17). If one truly repents, there will be some natural reforming, but that is not the whole of repentance.

Repentance is not just being religious. One may be very religious, in a sense, and never repent of his sins. The Pharisees were like that, and John the Baptist frankly told them he doubted their repentance was genuine (Matthew 3:7-10). Acts 8 contains the story of the conversion of a sorcerer named Simon (Acts 8:9-13). When Simon saw Philip performing miracles, he asked if he might have this ability and even offered money to buy the gift of the Holy Spirit (8:18-23). Peter's strong rebuking of Simon and his urging him to repent of this wickedness indicated that, although Simon appeared to be religious, he had not really repented. Being religious is not necessarily repentance.

What Repentance Is

Repentance is a change of will. The word "repentance" literally means "a change of mind," but it goes even deeper than that. It is a change of direction in the mind, heart and life. It is a conscious turning from sin and Satan and a turning to God.

The parable of the prodigal son in Luke 15 is perhaps the best biblical example of repentance. The son rebelled against his father and then wasted his inheritance in wild living. He fell so low he had to eat with pigs. But he came to his senses and decided to return home to tell his father, "I have sinned against heaven and against you" (Luke 15:18). This is godly sorrow that leads to repentance.

Then he went to his father, expressing sorrow for the life he had lived and asking for forgiveness. This is the fruit of repentance. True repentance is surrendering to God, a surrender that motivates us to change.

Repentance is obedience to God. The Bible repeatedly emphasizes the necessity of repentance if we are to obey God fully. Without repentance, all our religion, all our good works, all our good intentions or resolutions – all these things we may substitute for real repentance – are of no value whatsoever. Very plainly Jesus said, "Unless you repent, you will all perish" (Luke 13:3, 5).

The Role of Repentance in Salvation

Repentance is part of the gospel of Christ. On the day the church began, the first Pentecost after our Lord's resurrection, Peter preached the gospel of salvation through Christ (Acts 2). He concluded his message by saying, "Repent, and be baptized, every one of you, in the name of Jesus Christ for the forgiveness of your sins" (Acts 2:38). So, repentance is necessary and essential for sins to be forgiven.

God desperately wants us to repent of our sins, be baptized and be saved. Second Peter 3:9 reads, "He is patient with you, not wanting anyone to perish, but everyone to come to repentance."

In December 1993, the Bear Bryant Coach of the Year Award in college football was presented to Terry Bowden, the young first-year coach at Auburn University. Terry had taken a struggling program that was on probation and led his team to an undefeated season.

Interestingly, Terry's father, Bobby Bowden, the longtime successful coach at Florida State, was also nominated for the award. Much good-natured joking and teasing took place at the banquet between father and son as they waited to hear who had won the prestigious award.

Terry won, and in his acceptance speech he thanked his team, his fellow coaches, Auburn, and then his family.

"Let me tell you a story about my father," he said. "My parents always took us five kids to church. Even when we were on a trip, they took us to church. Once, while on vacation, we went to this church that was a little more emotional than we were used to. The minister was shouting and pounding the pulpit. He began to look around the congregation for someone to single out, and he spotted my father.

"Mom and Dad had marched us down to the front pew. Mom was on one end and Dad was on the other end with us five kids squeezed in between, to be sure we would behave in church. The preacher pointed dramatically to my dad and this conversation took place:

" 'You there. Do you have faith?'

" 'Yes, I have faith,' Dad answered.

" 'If I put a 2 x 4 board down there on the floor, do you have enough faith to walk across it?'

" 'Yes, I could do that,' Dad replied.

" 'But,' said the preacher, 'what if I took that same 2 x 4 board and placed it across the top of the two tallest buildings in New York City, would you have enough faith to walk across it then?'

" 'No, I don't have that much faith,' Dad admitted.

" 'But what if somebody were standing on the other end,' said the preacher, 'and was dangling one of your children off the side. Would you cross the board then?'

Terry said that his father turned and looked down the pew at his five fidgety kids and asked, 'Which one?' "

Of course, Terry was just kidding. Coach Bowden would have sacrificed his life for all his kids. But the point I want to make is this: Our loving, Father God does not say, "Which one? Which of My children should I lay my life on the line for?" He died for us and doesn't want anyone to perish, but everyone to come to repentance.

Repentance is not just a one-time act of salvation. Our repentance should be a deep, constant, ongoing attitude of humble submission before the Lord. Repentance is an everyday way of life. Every day we should be conscious of any presence of sin in our lives, and we should turn to God in prayer saying, "God, forgive me. I repent. Help me to overcome temptation. Help me to have a Christlike attitude toward others, and most importantly, toward You."

Talking Back

1. In your own words, define the concept of repentance.
2. What is the difference between worldly sorrow and godly sorrow? Can you think of times in your own life when you have had one or the other?
3. What is the difference between godly fear (respect) and simply being scared?
4. What is the difference between biblical repentance and reform?
5. What role does repentance play in our salvation?

Exercising Your Faith

Pray every day that God will give you an ongoing spirit of repentance. Recognize that repentance is an everyday way of life.

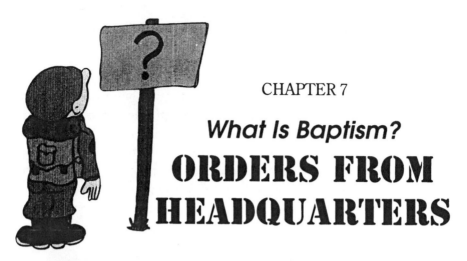

CHAPTER 7

What Is Baptism?
ORDERS FROM
HEADQUARTERS

The subject of baptism is one of the most controversial doctrines in religion. Bible believers have debated, argued and separated over baptism for centuries.

We have disagreed about who is to be baptized – infants or adults.

We have disagreed over how people should be baptized – by sprinkling or pouring water on a person's head or completely immersing the person in water.

We have disagreed over why one should be baptized – as a symbol of our salvation or as a necessary point of receiving salvation.

We have disagreed over when a person should be baptized – after a waiting period or immediately upon believing in Christ.

Without a doubt, many people would say, "Why all this fuss about baptism? It's only a religious ceremony, isn't it? What difference does it make?"

The short answer is, "All the difference in the world!"

This chapter and the next will focus only on what the Bible has to say about baptism. If we want to know who Jesus was, what He taught and what He commanded His followers to do, we must go to the Bible for answers. To look elsewhere is to rely on the opinions or traditions of men, and that is insufficient. We are only interested in the truth concerning baptism as defined in the Bible.

We will study this vitally important topic by asking four questions:

1. What is baptism?
2. How is baptism performed?
3. Why should we be baptized?
4. Who should be baptized?

What Is Baptism?

Baptism is the full immersion in water of a believer for the forgiveness of sins. It is an identification with the death, burial and resurrection of Jesus Christ. It was commanded by Jesus and is essential for entrance into His spiritual body, the church.

Baptism is a spiritual cleansing of one's soul by the power of the blood of Christ, not water. Baptism is the point of beginning for a person's new life in Christ. It gives one the right to wear the name Christian.

How the Bible Describes Baptism

Perhaps looking at how the Bible describes baptism will help us understand what baptism is like.

Baptism is like being washed from sin.

> And now what are you waiting for? Get up, be baptized and wash your sins away, calling on his name (Acts 22:16).

As Paul recounted his own salvation experience, he said that his teacher, Ananias, told him to "be baptized and wash your sins away." So, baptism is like washing something to make it clean. God uses the water of baptism as a spiritual cleanser. The water itself has no power. But God has chosen to make our obedience to the command to be baptized in water the means by which we demonstrate our faith, and on that basis, He cleanses us.

It is very important to note in Acts 22 that although Paul had believed in Jesus and was showing his true faith and repentance by three days of fasting and praying, he was still in his sins, and needed them washed away in baptism.

Baptism is like putting on new clothes.

> [F]or all of you who were baptized into Christ have clothed yourself with Christ (Galatians 3:27).

Perhaps one time you were wearing dirty, grimy, smelly clothes. When you had the opportunity to clean up and put on clean clothes, you probably felt like a whole new person. In a similar sense, when a person is baptized into Christ, he wears new clothing, the righteousness of Christ. Before baptism, we are wearing the old clothes of sin; then, at baptism, we lay those clothes aside, and wear Christ as our new spiritual clothing.

Baptism is like a burial and a resurrection.

What shall we say, then? Shall we go on sinning so that grace may increase? By no means! We died to sin; how can we live in it any longer? Or don't you know that all of us who were baptized into Christ Jesus were baptized into his death? We were therefore buried with him through baptism into death in order that, just as Christ was raised from the dead through the glory of the Father, we too may live a new life.

If we have been united with him like this in his death, we will certainly also be united with him in his resurrection. For we know that our old self was crucified with him so that the body of sin might be done away with that we should no longer be slaves to sin (Romans 6:1-6).

What truths do we learn from this passage?

1. The burial of baptism signified that we died to sin. Just as a body dies before it is buried, and as Christ died before He was buried, through complete obedience (faith, repentance and baptism), we, too, die to sin. This does not mean that all temptation is gone or that we will live the new life to perfection. It means that we now have a Savior who forgives our sins.

2. Baptism buries the old self. After a death, there must be a burial. Jesus died and was buried, and so are we through baptism. The burial by immersion in water associates us with Jesus' death and burial in which He gave His life for our sins.

3. Baptism signified our being raised to live a new life. Christ was raised from the dead and we are raised, spiritually speaking, to begin a new life. So baptism is similar to Christ's own death, burial and resurrection. It is a dying to the former control of sin and a resurrection to the new life in Christ.

Baptism is like moving from one world to another.

For Christ died for sins once for all, the righteous for the unrighteous, to bring you to God. He was put to death in the body but made alive by the Spirit, through whom also he went and preached to the spirits in prison who disobeyed long ago when God waited patiently in the days of Noah while the ark was being built. In it only a few people, eight in all, were saved through water, and this water symbolizes baptism that now saves you also – not the removal of dirt from the body but the pledge of a good conscience toward God. It saves you by the resurrection of Jesus Christ (1 Peter 3:18-21).

How did water save Noah? God used water to transport Noah from a world of sin to a new world of purity. In a similar way, Peter says the water of baptism is the divine means by which God transports a person from sin to purity, from lost sinner to saved child of God. In this transferring process, Peter says that baptism saves you. If baptism saves, then before baptism, one must be lost. Until baptism transports us out of sin and disobedience, one is lost. However, at baptism, God transports the true believer into a new position as His child.

Baptism is like being born again.

Now there was a man of the Pharisees named Nicodemus, a member of the Jewish ruling council. He came to Jesus at night and said, "Rabbi, we know you are a teacher who has come from God. For no one could perform the miraculous signs you are doing if God were not with him."

In reply Jesus declared, "I tell you the truth, no one can see the kingdom of God unless he is born again."

"How can a man be born when he is old?" Nicodemus asked. "Surely he cannot enter a second time into his mother's womb to be born!"

Jesus answered, "I tell you the truth, no one can enter the kingdom of God unless he is born of water and the Spirit" (John 3:1-5).

[H]e saved us, not because of righteous things we had done, but because of his mercy. He saved us through the washing of rebirth and renewal by the Holy Spirit (Titus 3:5).

Just as the birth of a child marks the time when that child is now considered a part of the family, baptism is the time in which one is born again into the family of God, "born of water and the Spirit," Jesus said.

How Is Baptism Performed?

The word "baptism" in the original Greek language means "immersion." Each time baptism is described, it is seen as going down into the water and coming up out of the water. There are at least four reasons why the only valid baptism is by immersion, not sprinkling or pouring:

1. The word "baptism" or "baptize" literally means to dip, immerse or plunge. As used in Scripture, the word always referred to full immersion in water, a burial as Romans 6 describes it.

2. Biblical examples of baptism were complete immersion. When Philip baptized the Ethiopian eunuch, they went down into the water (Acts 8:38). The baptism took place, and then both men "came up out of the water" (v. 39).

3. Baptism is a picture of the death, burial and resurrection of Christ, as we noticed in Romans 6. This burial in water means a literal immersion, submerged below water.

4. The words sprinkle and pour never appear in Scripture in connection with baptism. Neither is there a biblical example of sprinkling or pouring for baptism. However, baptism is repeatedly described in the New Testament as the occasion where God applies the saving and cleansing blood of Christ to our souls.

This last thought leads us into two very important questions that will be examined in the next chapter: "Why should we be baptized?" and "Who should be baptized?"

Talking Back

1. How does baptism save us, according to 1 Peter 3:21?

2. Which analogy in the "Baptism is like ..." segment was most interesting to you and why?

3. Reflecting on Romans 6:1-6, consider these four questions:

   a. How is baptism like a death?

   b. How is baptism like a burial?

   c. How is baptism like a resurrection?

   d. What does this passage teach you about baptism?

4. How is baptism like a birth?

5. How would you explain to someone that Bible baptism is immersion not just sprinkling or pouring?

Exercising Your Faith

Interview someone who has been baptized recently. Ask these questions: Why were you baptized? How did you feel during your baptism? What have you experienced since your baptism?

CHAPTER 8

Why Should We Be Baptized?

I SURRENDER

O nce there was a mother bird who decided to teach her baby birdies how to build a nest. She started her lesson by saying, "To build a nest you must first find a secluded spot." One of the little birds flew off immediately. The mother bird was sad, but she did have the others to teach.

"Then you need to find some straw," Mother Bird said. Another bird flew off. The mother continued, "To build a nest, you also need some mud. You must mix the straw and mud together." Still another bird flew off. Then the mother demonstrated to the only remaining bird how to form the mud and straw into a nest.

Later each bird was found, and each claimed to have made a nest. The first bird called his secluded spot a nest. The second bird had only a pile of straw which he called a nest. The third bird had straw and mud rolled together in a ball and was calling it a nest. Only the last bird had made a genuine nest. The others had essential elements of a nest, but not a nest.

So it is with obeying all of Christ's commands concerning salvation. A person may have faith only and say he has obeyed Christ. Another person may have only repented and say he has obeyed Christ. Still another person may have only been baptized and say he has obeyed Christ. But the New testament puts these three – faith, repentance and baptism – together as essential for building one's nest of salvation.

In Chapter 7 we discussed two questions: "What is baptism?" and "How is baptism performed." Now we will look at two more: "Why should we be baptized?" and "Who should be baptized?"

Why Should We Be Baptized?

We should be baptized for the forgiveness or remission of sins.

> Repent and be baptized, every one of you, in the name of Jesus Christ for the forgiveness of your sins. And you will receive the gift of the Holy Spirit (Acts 2:38).

> Go into all the world and preach the good news to all creation. Whoever believes and is baptized will be saved, but whoever does not believe will be condemned (Mark 16:15-16).

> And now what are you waiting for? Get up, be baptized and wash your sins away, calling on his name (Acts 22:16).

> [A]nd this water symbolizes baptism that now saves you also – not the removal of dirt from the body but a pledge of a good conscience toward God (1 Peter 3:21).

These passages speak clearly concerning the connection between baptism and salvation. In Scripture, every time that God saw fit to connect baptism and salvation, the order is always baptism, then salvation.

Many people sincerely believe that salvation occurs prior to baptism, as soon as one believes. But that is confusing the means of salvation with the occasion of salvation. Faith is the means of salvation, but baptism is the occasion where the blood of Jesus washes our sins away and gives us forgiveness of those sins.

We should be baptized to get into Christ.

> [F]or all of you who were baptized into Christ have clothed yourself with Christ (Galatians 3:27).

> Or don't you know that all of us who were baptized into Christ Jesus were baptized into his death? We were therefore buried with him through baptism into death in order that, just as Christ was raised from the dead through the glory of the Father, we too may live a new life (Romans 6:3-4).

To be in Christ means to be united with Christ or in fellowship with Christ. Many blessings are to be found in Christ:

1. There is no condemnation for those in Christ (Romans 8:1).

2. One who is in Christ is a new creation (2 Corinthians 5:17).

3. In Christ, we have redemption, the forgiveness of sin (Colossians 1:14).

4. In Christ, we have every spiritual blessing (Ephesians 1:3).

All of these blessings and more are found in Christ. Now the obvious question is, how does one get *into* Christ? Romans 6:3 and Galatians 3:27 teach that we get into Christ by being baptized into Christ. Consider this question: If the very instant I believe in Jesus I am in union with Christ, how could I later be baptized into Christ?

The Word of God doesn't teach such an absurdity. The Bible teaches that by faith, followed by baptism and accompanied by repentance, we are brought into union with Christ.

Perhaps this illustration will help. I knew my wife several months before we ever started dating. We liked each other as friends, but both of us were dating other people and had no unifying commitment to one another. As time progressed, we began dating and spending a lot of time together, eventually falling in love.

Were we married at this point? Of course not. The relationship had not yet been changed by the occasion of a wedding ceremony.

Over the course of several months, we stopped dating other people and became engaged. Certainly we believed in one another and had experienced a change of heart about ourselves and others. A radical change in lifestyle is apparent.

Were we married yet? No, a change of lifestyle and priorities is essential to a good marriage, but it's not enough.

Our wedding date finally arrived, and the wedding ceremony was performed. We repeated our vows, exchanged rings and were pronounced husband and wife.

Were we married yet? Yes!

We weren't married when our hearts changed, when we fell in love and believed in one another as future life partners (that's belief).

We weren't married when our lives and priorities changed (that's repentance).

We were married on the occasion when the relationship changed (that's baptism).

The wedding ceremony changed neither our hearts (belief) nor our lives (repentance), but it was the occasion that changed the relationship!

Or take the case of citizenship. Becoming a citizen of a country requires a change in beliefs and behaviors, but the actual change from a non-citizen to a citizen occurs only at the initiation ceremony.

Becoming the president of the United States involves being elected in November and undergoing changes in beliefs and behaviors, but the actual change from being an ordinary citizen to the president occurs only at the occasion of the Jan. 20 inauguration ceremony.

These kinds of illustrations could continue, but the point is the single act (wedding ceremony, initiation, inauguration, baptism, etc.) is the occasion of transferring from one position to another. Although changed beliefs and behaviors are essential, they are not the same as the actual placement into the new position.

We must not confuse the roles and reasons for faith, repentance and baptism. Being in Christ requires faith and repentance, but the occasion where we have our sins washed away and receive forgiveness of sins is baptism.

We should be baptized to obey God. Baptism for the forgiveness of sins is repeatedly given in the New Testament as a commandment from God. There is no power in the water. The power is in the obedience to God's command. We do not believe or teach water salvation. We believe and teach salvation by simple obedience to God's commands to believe in Jesus as the Son of God and confess Him as our Lord, to repent of our sins and be baptized into Christ for the forgiveness of our sins!

Who Should Not Be Baptized?

Let's consider some improper candidates for baptism.

People with insincere belief. Constantine the Great, emperor of the Roman Empire during the fourth century, decided that since Christians were generally of good character, all in the Roman Empire should be baptized as Christians. He even had his armies baptized. Many, of course, were insincere and not really believers. Only those who have come to a conviction about their sins ("cut to the heart," Acts 2:37) and who express sincere faith in Jesus Christ as their Savior and Lord should be baptized.

Infants or young children incapable of understanding the gospel. Infants and young children have no conviction of sin. They are incapable of exercising faith, repentance and confession. Infant baptism, sprinkling or pouring of water on infants, was begun by the Roman Catholic Church centuries after the establishment of the New Testament church in Acts, and it is entirely unbiblical.

People with improper or impure motives. Some people have become Christians to please a family member, to help their business, to save their marriage, etc. Only those who are serious about following Jesus, those with pure hearts and motives, should be baptized into Christ.

People who are exclusively trusting baptism for salvation. Baptism alone will not save any more than faith alone or repentance alone will save. Baptism is not a "work for your own righteousness" type of act. It is an act of obedience.

Who Should Be Baptized?

Everyone mature enough in his or her own thinking to understand the teaching of the gospel to repent of their sins, confess Jesus as Lord and demonstrate faith in Jesus as their Savior is a proper candidate.

Baptism completes a person's salvation. Failure to be baptized into Christ is disobedience to God's clear commands in Scripture. If you have not completed your salvation by being buried with Christ in baptism for the forgiveness of sins, why not do so immediately?

Talking Back

1. Review Acts 2:36-38. What does this passage teach about the necessity of baptism?

2. How could a person be "baptized into Christ" if he or she were already "in Christ" by just believing in Him?

3. Three factors change a person's relationship to Christ:

   a. What does belief change?

   b. What does repentance change?

   c. What does baptism change?

4. Why are infants or small children not candidates for baptism?

5. If someone asked you, "Why should I be baptized?", how would you answer?

Exercising Your Faith

Looking back at your own baptism, how do you feel about it? What do you remember about it?

If you have not been baptized, why not? Pray that God will lead you to complete obedience of His will.

CHAPTER 9

The Lord's Supper
IN MEMORIAM

I magine with me for just a moment that you were in the U.S. Army and had been stationed in a combat zone. One of your best friends in the army was patrolling alongside you one day when an enemy soldier tossed a hand grenade in your direction. Your friend pushed you out of harm's way and threw himself on the grenade, sacrificing his life to save your life.

A few weeks later you receive a notice from your friend's parents inviting you to a memorial service in his honor. Would you attend? Of course you would.

Jesus Christ gave His life for you to save you from eternal death. And His Father, God, has invited you to a memorial service for Him every Sunday. That memorial service is called "communion" or the "Lord's Supper." Our attendance and participation in this memorial are a small sacrifice to make for the One who made the total sacrifice for us!

Memory is so important. There are many people, places, events and truths we should remember. We leave ourselves notes or make lists about things we should remember to get done. We save pictures to remind us of trips or events. We build memorials to people or events we want to remember.

The word "memorial" comes from the same root word as the word "memory." A memorial is something that stirs our memory of a past event. The Lord's Supper is a memorial that allows us to remember what Jesus did for us at the Cross.

"Do this in remembrance of me," Jesus said of the bread representing His body and the cup representing His blood – the two elements that make up the memorial we know as communion or the Lord's Supper.

God knows how forgetful we can be so He sets reminders in our path to help us remember important truths:

The Passover. The Passover Feast was a memorial observed by the children of Israel to remember God's delivering the Hebrews from centuries of Egyptian captivity and slavery:

> Obey these instructions as a lasting ordinance for you and your descendants. When you enter the land that the Lord will give you as he promised, observe this ceremony. And when your children ask you, "What does this ceremony mean to you?" then tell them, "It is the Passover sacrifice to the Lord, who passed over the houses of the Israelites in Egypt and spared our homes when he struck down the Egyptians." Then the people bowed down and worshiped (Exodus 12:24-27).

This annual memorial served not only to remind the older folks of God's deliverance but also to teach the younger folks about God's care and provision for His people.

The jar of manna. God fed these same people during their wanderings in the wilderness toward the Promised Land of Canaan with manna, bread from heaven. God wanted His people to remember His care for them so He commanded them to keep a jar of manna for future generations to see (Exodus 16:32-33).

The 12 stones. In Joshua 4, the Israelites were preparing to cross the Jordan River into Canaan. Twelve men, representing each tribe, were to bring a stone from the bed of the river and set them together for an altar to the Lord. These stones were to serve as a memorial to Israel, reminding them of how God had allowed them miraculously to cross the Jordan River (Joshua 4:5-7).

The Lord's Supper. It should come as no surprise, considering the history of God's memorials, that the Lord instituted a memorial for us to remember His sacrifice for us. Jesus said, "[D]o this in remembrance of Me" (Luke 22:19).

How Was the Lord's Supper Instituted?

Jesus was with His disciples in the Upper Room just before He was arrested, placed on trial and crucified. It was the time of the Passover Feast for the Jews. As Jesus observed the Passover Feast with His disciples, He began to instruct them concerning a new memorial feast that would have two elements:

The bread.

> While they were eating, Jesus took bread, gave thanks and broke it, and gave it to his disciples, saying, "Take and eat; this is my body" (Matthew 26:26).

The eating of this bread is to remind us of His body. It is a memorial to Christ's sacrificial death.

The fruit of the vine, the cup.

> Then he took the cup, gave thanks and offered it to them, saying, "Drink from it, all of you. This is my blood of the covenant, which is poured out for many for the forgiveness of sins. I tell you, I will not drink of this fruit of the vine from now on until that day when I drink it anew with you in my Father's kingdom" (Matthew 26:27-29).

The drinking of this fruit of the vine both reminds us and teaches us. It reminds us of Jesus' ultimate sacrifice of shedding His blood for us. It helps to teach us that only through the shed blood of Christ can we have forgiveness of sins.

What Exactly Is the Lord's Supper?

The Lord's Supper is a living memorial to Christ. All attention should be on Christ as we remember the Cross and celebrate the freedom from sin He bought for us with His own blood. The Lord's Supper may represent many things to us, but it is always Jesus' appointed way for us to remember Him.

The Lord's Supper is a time of thanksgiving. Before distributing the bread and the cup, Jesus gave thanks. When Christians give thanks for the bread and the cup during the Lord's Supper, we are imitating Jesus. We are also expressing gratitude for all that God has done for us through Christ.

The Lord's Supper is a communion, a fellowship with other Christians. It signifies that we hold something in common as we participate, or commune, together. In communion, a Christian can share alongside another Christian regardless of economic, social, cultural or racial differences. Communion expresses, as almost nothing else can, our acceptance of one another as equals before Christ. It is an active participation in sharing and fellowship:

> Is not the cup of thanksgiving for which we give thanks a participation in the blood of Christ? And is not the bread that we break a participation in the body of Christ? (1 Corinthians 10:16).

The Lord's Supper is a celebration of hope. Paul wrote,

> For whenever you eat this bread and drink this cup, you proclaim the Lord's death until he comes (1 Corinthians 11:26).

So the Lord's Supper not only recalls the past (Christ's sacrificial death) and unifies the present (as we commune and fellowship together), but it also looks to the future when the Lord will come again for His faithful children.

When Should We Take the Lord's Supper?

In the New Testament we learn that the early church was observing the Lord's Supper "on the first day of the week" (Acts 20:7). This is a biblical example for us to follow so we observe communion each Sunday, the first day of the week.

Is that too much to ask of us?

The real question should be, "Why don't all churches observe communion every Sunday?"

All churches give each Sunday. First Corinthians 16:2 indicates that we are to give on the first day of the week, the same phrase that describes when we are to commune around the Lord's table. Given the biblical evidence, why would anyone do one and not the other?

We should observe the Lord's Supper every first day of the week, every Sunday.

How Should We Observe the Lord's Supper?

First Corinthians 11:20-30 tells us something about the proper observation of communion:

> When you come together, it is not the Lord's Supper you eat, for as you eat, each of you goes ahead without waiting for anybody else. One remains hungry, another gets drunk. Don't you have homes to eat and drink in? Or do you despise the church of God and humiliate those who have nothing? What shall I say to you? Shall I praise you for this? Certainly not!
>
> For I received from the Lord what I also passed on to you: The Lord Jesus, on the night he was betrayed, took bread, and when he had given thanks, he broke it and said, "This is my body, which is for you; do this in remembrance of me." In the same way, after supper he took the cup saying, "This cup is the new covenant in my blood; do this, whenever you drink it, in remembrance of me." For whenever you eat this bread and drink this cup, you proclaim the Lord's death until he comes.
>
> Therefore, whoever eats the bread or drinks the cup of the Lord in an unworthy manner will be guilty of sinning against the body and blood of the Lord. A man ought to examine himself before he eats of the bread and drinks of the cup. For anyone who eats and drinks without recognizing the body of the Lord eats and drinks judgment on himself. That is why many among you are weak and sick, and a number of you have fallen asleep.

The Corinthian Christians were faithful enough in regularly observing communion, but they were also abusing it. They were combining the communion with a large meal, and some were rudely eating and drinking to excess while others were being ignored. Some were apparently even turning this celebration into a large party.

Paul scolded the abusers for partaking in an unworthy manner. He also left some instructions for proper administration of the Lord's Supper:

1. The communion should be done in remembrance of Jesus (vv. 24-25).

2. We should recognize the serious consequences of partaking in an unworthy manner (vv. 27-29).

3. We are to examine ourselves as we partake (v. 28).

4. Spiritual and/or physical sickness can be the result of abusing the Lord's Supper (vv. 29-30).

Some Suggestions to Partake of the Lord's Supper in a Worthy Manner

Humans are prone to forgetfulness. We tend to forget everything from addresses to anniversaries. But we cannot afford to forget some things, and the Lord's Supper should be at the top of that list.

Remember each Sunday that what we are doing when we gather around the communion table is not ritual; it is a memorial done in remembrance of Christ. Here are some suggestions to help as you partake:

- Read carefully, discerningly and prayerfully some Scriptures dealing with communion or the Cross, such as 1 Corinthians 11:20-30; Mark 14:12-25 and Isaiah 53, while the Lord's Supper is being passed.
- Reflect on the words of a meaningful hymn that deals with communion or the Cross such as "He Paid a Debt," "Boundless Love," "The Old Rugged Cross" or "When I Survey the Wondrous Cross."
- Bow your head, shut the world out and pray. Concentrate on and be thankful for our Lord's great sacrifice for us.

Talking Back

1. What memorials have you visited or attended? (the Washington Monument, the Lincoln Memorial, Baseball Hall of Fame, a funeral service)

2. What is the point or purpose of memorials? In what way is the Lord's Supper a memorial?

3. What is the meaning and significance of the bread and the fruit of the vine?

4. How were the Corinthian Christians abusing the Lord's Supper? In what ways can we abuse the Lord's Supper today?

5. How can we better discipline ourselves to partake of communion in a worthy manner?

Exercising Your Faith

Go over the list of suggestions on partaking of communion properly and resolve to try them next Sunday morning during communion.

CHAPTER 10

Prayer

TWO-WAY COMMUNICATION

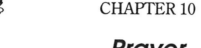

A small Kentucky town had two churches and one whiskey distillery. Members of both churches complained that the distillery gave the community a bad image. On top of this the owner of the distillery was an atheist. Church members had tried to shut down the place but were unsuccessful.

Finally, the two churches decided to hold a joint Saturday night prayer meeting. They would ask for God to intervene. Saturday night came, and all through the prayer meeting a vicious electrical storm raged. To the delight of the church members, lightning struck the distillery and burned it to the ground.

The next morning sermons in both churches were about "The Power of Prayer." Fire insurance adjusters promptly notified the distillery owner that they would not pay for his damages. The fire was caused by an act of God they said, and coverage for acts of God were excluded in the policy.

The distillery owner promptly sued the churches, claiming they had conspired with God to destroy the building. The churches absolutely denied that they had done anything to cause the fire. The trial judge observed: "I find one thing about this case that is very perplexing. We have a situation where the plaintiff, an atheist, is professing his belief in the power of prayer, and the defendants, the church members, are denying the power of prayer!"

I am afraid that all too often Christians deny the power of prayer. It is impossible to be a powerful Christian apart from prayer. God speaks to us through His inspired Word, and we talk to God through prayer. If we don't pray regularly or faithfully, we have cut off half the communication line between us and God.

One of our regular prayers should be, "Lord, teach us to pray," as the disciples requested of Jesus. We can always learn how to pray more effectively and more in the will of God. We shall examine these important questions about prayer: "What is prayer?" "What is its purpose?" "Why should we pray?" and "How can we learn to pray more effectively?"

What Is Prayer?

The answer to this question can be found in Matthew 6:9-13, the pattern Jesus gave us to use as a model in our prayer life:

> Our Father in heaven,
> hallowed be your name,
> your kingdom come,
> your will be done on earth as it is in heaven.
> Give us today our daily bread.
> Forgive us our debts,
> as we also have forgiven our debtors.
> And lead us not into temptation,
> but deliver us from the evil one.

Prayer is worship. "Our Father in heaven, hallowed be your name." In prayer, on bended knee literally or figuratively, we come before our holy and righteous Father with a worshipful spirit.

Prayer is submission. "Your will be done on earth as it is in heaven." Prayer is submitting all of our life to the will of God. It means we make Him the Boss and are willing to yield to His will in every area of our lives.

Prayer is asking God for something. "Give us this day our daily bread." Prayer is presenting our requests to God and asking Him to grant them.

> Ask and it will be given to you; seek and you will find; knock and the door will be opened to you. For everyone who asks receives; he who seeks finds; and to him who knocks, the door will be opened.
> Which of you, if his son asks for bread, will give him a

stone? Or if he asks for a fish, will give him a snake? If you, then, though you are evil, know how to give good gifts to your children, how much more will your Father in heaven give good gifts to those who ask him! (Matthew 7:7-11).

You want something but don't get it. You kill and covet, but you cannot have what you want. You quarrel and fight. You do not have, because you do not ask God (James 4:2).

Prayer is confession and forgiveness. "Forgive us out debts, as we also have forgiven our debtors." We confess our sins and ask forgiveness from God in prayer, and that forgiveness from God can be dependent upon our having a forgiving attitude toward others:

For if you forgive men when they sin against you, your heavenly Father will also forgive you. But if you do not forgive men their sins, your Father will not forgive your sins (Matthew 6:14-15).

Prayer is resisting temptation. "And lead us not into temptation, but deliver us from the evil one." This was the same counsel Jesus later gave His disciples in the shadow of the Cross: "Watch and pray so that you will not fall into temptation" (Matthew 26:41). In prayer, we run from temptation and to God for His strength and protection from Satan.

How to Have a Meaningful Prayer Life

Set aside a regular time for prayer. Look forward to that time of prayer as you would an appointment with an important person, which of course, it is. Having a regular and consistent time to pray provides a pattern of spiritual discipline that can be helpful to spiritual growth.

Pray conversationally rather than formally. We should learn how to be at home with God and be comfortable going into His presence, just as a child does with a loving father. There are several benefits of conversational prayer:

1. It is the best way to obey the words of 1 Thessalonians 5:17: "Pray continually."

2. You can be as long or as short in prayer as need be, praying while sitting at a red light, waiting in line, etc.

3. You can focus on your relationship not just words. The bottom line in prayer is that God wants a relationship with us. Formality can hinder such a relationship. The only thing that will work is personally drawing closer to God, as a son to a father.

Avoid showy prayers and repetitious or cliché-filled prayers. Prayer should be genuine, heartfelt and intensely personal. Jesus said:

> But when you pray, do not be like the hypocrites, for they love to pray standing in the synagogues and on the street corners to be seen by men. I tell you the truth, they have received their reward in full. But when you pray, go into your room, close the door and pray to your Father, who is unseen. Then your Father, who sees what is done in secret, will reward you. And when you pray, do not keep on babbling like pagans, for they think they will be heard because of their many words. Do not be like them, for your Father knows what you need before you ask him (Matthew 6:5-8).

Pray unselfishly. We must not be selfish in prayer. We must not pray with improper motives:

> You want something but don't get it. You kill and covet, but you cannot have what you want. You quarrel and fight. You do not have, because you do not ask God. When you ask, you do not receive, because you ask with wrong motives, that you may spend what you get on your pleasures (James 4:2-3).

Our craving and desire in prayer should be primarily for the power of God and for His blessings upon us so we can better serve Him and others.

Developing a Powerful Prayer Life

The A-C-T-S plan of prayer. Designed to improve the quality and quantity of one's prayer life, the acronym A-C-T-S makes it simple to remember.

1. Begin prayer with adoration (Psalm 8; 1 Chronicles 29:10-13). Just adore God for His salvation, His blessings, His power, His glory, etc.

2. Continue in prayer with confession (James 5:13-16; Proverbs 28:13). Private sin is best confessed privately in your daily prayers. Simply confess to God your specific sins and pray for strength to overcome whatever temptation you are struggling with at the time.

3. Move on in prayer with thanksgiving (Philippians 4:6). Remember to thank God for whatever blessings you are receiving, lessons you are being taught, opportunities you are experiencing, etc.

4. Conclude in prayer with supplications or requests (Matthew 7:7-8; John 14:13). Make whatever request you desire from God. Pray about your needs, desires, goals and plans. In general, "present your requests to God" (Philippians 4:6).

The prayer of the heart. This concept is both biblical and practical and has really helped me personally:

1. The basic practice of the prayer of the heart involves selecting a word, a phrase or a Scripture, and repeating it several times, planting it deeply within yourself. You repeat it several times during the day. The idea is to have a prayer going on within you that you can notice at any time.

2. In choosing your prayer of the heart, you might select a short word that represents your heart's desire for that day, such as "joy," "peace," "patience" or "kindness." You repeat the word (or prayer phrase you compose) over and over again, so that it is planted within you as a deposit from which God can work to produce spiritual dividends in your life.

3. I will often choose a verse of Scripture and repeat it several times in the morning. Here are a few of my favorite prayer of the heart scriptures:

> Trust in the Lord with all your heart and lean not on your own understanding; in all your ways acknowledge him, and he will make your paths straight (Proverbs 3:5-6).

I may use all of the verse or only the part of it that I need most that day, such as, "Trust in the Lord" or "lean not on your own understanding."

> Create in me a pure heart, O God, and renew a steadfast spirit within me (Psalm 51:10).

> Rejoice in the Lord always. I will say it again: Rejoice! (Philippians 4:4).

> Do not be anxious about anything, but in everything, by prayer and petition, with thanksgiving, present your requests to God. And the peace of God, which transcends all understanding, will guard your hearts and your minds in Christ Jesus (Philippians 4:6-7).

This scripture is probably my most frequently used prayer of the heart, either all of it or portions of it, such as "Don't be anxious," or "Give me a spirit of thanksgiving," or "Give me a peace that guards my heart and mind, Lord."

4. The prayer of the heart is the best aid I have found to help me obey 1 Thessalonians 5:17: "pray continually." It is a continual prayer, creating a constant sense of openness to God and intimacy with God. I challenge you to try it!

Prayer is a spiritual discipline that produces spiritual growth. Aids like the prayer of the heart and the A-C-T-S plan can assist us in developing a powerful prayer life and a close personal relationship with the Lord.

No one should ever force a particular kind of prayer aid on another, but aids often help us to be more productive and regular in our prayer life. However you choose to pray, the main thing to remember is this: Pray regularly, consistently and with faith!

When we fail to do so, we shut down the communication line to God, and that is disastrous to the Christian life. So, as Paul wrote, "pray continually."

Talking Back

1. How often do you pray?

2. When you don't pray as much as you should or would like to, what is the reason? How could that be changed?

3. What is the most important truth you learned about prayer in this chapter?

4. How do you think we can best obey the command to "pray continually"?

5. Discuss some times when God answered prayers in your life. How did that make you feel, and how did it strengthen your faith?

Exercising Your Faith

Pick one of the aids for effective prayer mentioned in this chapter and begin to practice it. Especially try the prayer of the heart.

CHAPTER 11

Singing

SOUND OFF!

S inging has always been a meaningful way to worship God. It is amazing how many significant Bible events were characterized by singing:

- As the children of Israel crossed the Red Sea, escaping Egyptian bondage, they celebrated by worshiping God in song, a song Moses' sister, Miriam, composed.
- Hannah sang a song of thanksgiving at the birth of Samuel.
- At the death of King Saul, David, his successor, composed a song.
- Psalm 45 was written to celebrate a wedding.
- An entire book of the Old Testament, the Song of Solomon or Song of Songs, is devoted to a song. In fact, 1 Kings 4:32 says that Solomon wrote 1,005 songs!
- Four hymns are recorded in Luke 1-2, accompanying the birth of Jesus.
- Revelation 5:9 says the saints in heaven are singing a new song and someday we will join them.
- Approximately 150 songs are recorded in the Bible.

It is easy to see the great emphasis Scripture places on singing. Undoubtedly, one reason is that God knows the tremendous influence music has on our lives. Music has often been called the universal language. We have music in our homes, cars, offices, stores, schools, restaurants and even our churches. Music has the capacity to:

Inspire and motivate us. "The Star-Spangled Banner" and "God Bless America" inspire Americans to greater patriotism.

Hymns and devotional songs have long motivated and inspired Christians in spiritual living.

Control moods. Retail stores and restaurants play mood music that, in a very subtle way, leaves a favorable impression on people. And, of course, we know that music is the language of love.

Catch our attention and stick in our minds. Have you ever found yourself humming the jingle from a TV commercial? Have you ever found yourself singing a song all day that you heard on the radio that morning? These kinds of instances are evidence of music's subtle effect on the mind.

Call people to action. School alma maters call students and alumni to action. When I was playing high school football, I remember how charged up the players were when the alma mater was sung at the pep rally. Soldiers in every war have gone off to battle to the tunes of music that suggest a cause worth defending.

If you stop to think about it, the influence that music has on our everyday lives is tremendous. We celebrate with a song. We mourn with a song. We relax with a song. We entertain with a song. God knew that music would play an important role in our lives, so we also worship with a song.

Why Is A Cappella Singing Used in Worship?

One of the first things visitors usually notice when they visit a church of Christ is the absence of musical instruments in our worship assemblies. There are two primary reasons why we do not use instruments:

1. The first reason is the Bible authorizes singing but the New Testament is silent concerning the accompaniment of our singing by musical instruments. It seems that the safest and surest route is to practice what is authorized by Scripture (singing) and avoid adding to the Word of God where it is silent. Only five scriptures deal with church music in the New Testament. Let's take a brief look at all five.

Speak to one another with psalms, hymns and spiritual songs. Sing and make music in your heart to the Lord (Ephesians 5:19).

In Ephesians 5:19 we are authorized to do three things: speak in psalms, hymns and spiritual songs; sing; and make music in our hearts.

> Let the word of Christ dwell in you richly as you teach and admonish one another with all wisdom, and as you sing psalms, hymns and spiritual songs with gratitude in your hearts to God (Colossians 3:16).

In this Colossians passage, we are also authorized to do three things: teach with psalms, hymns and spiritual songs; admonish; and sing with gratitude in our hearts to God.

> So what shall I do? I will pray with my spirit, but I will also pray with my mind; I will sing with my spirit, but I will also sing with my mind (1 Corinthians 14:15).

This passage in 1 Corinthians instructs us to sing with spirit and understanding of what we are singing.

> I will declare your name to my brothers; in the presence of the congregation I will sing your praises (Hebrews 2:12).

This verse in Hebrews 2 speaks only of singing praises in the congregation.

> Through Jesus, therefore, let us continually offer to God a sacrifice of praise – the fruit of lips that confess his name (Hebrews 13:15).

Hebrews 13:15 lets us know we can worship through the fruit of our lips.

So, the primary reason we do not have musical instruments in our worship assemblies is the conviction that the Bible does not authorize their use.

2. The second reason we do not use instruments is a practical and historical reason. It is a well-established historical fact that musical instruments were not introduced into any formal worship until at least the seventh century – more than 600 years after the church was established on the day of Pentecost.

> The organ is said to have been first introduced into church music by Pope Vitalian I in A.D. 666. In A.D. 757, a great

organ was sent as a present to Pepin, King of the Franks, by the Byzantine emperor, Constantine Copronymus, and placed in the church of St. Corneille at Compiegne. Soon after Charlemagne's time, organs became common (*Chambers Encyclopedia*, Vol. 7, p. 112).

John Calvin, founder of the Presbyterian denomination, said,

Musical instruments in celebrating the praises of God would be no more suitable than the burning of incense, the lighting of lamps, and the restoration of the other shadows of the law. The Papists, therefore, have foolishly borrowed this, as well as many other things, from the Jews. Men who are fond of outward pomp may delight in that noise; but the simplicity which God recommends to us by the apostles is far more pleasing to him" (*John Calvin's Commentary*, Thirty-third Psalm).

Musical instruments were not used or endorsed by the first-century church as described in the Bible. That historical fact seems to be a very strong practical reason to not use them in our worship assemblies.

How Can We Please God with Our Worship in Song?

First of all, sing! We are commanded to sing praises to God – it is not optional. Singing is no more optional than praying or partaking of the Lord's Supper. God loves to hear His children's voices. All our voices sound beautiful to the One who created them.

Sing with understanding. We should concentrate on the words we are singing for 1 Corinthians 14:15 instructs us to sing with our minds or with understanding. Sometimes more emphasis and attention are given to the melody of a song than to the words. People may sing without thinking about the words. God cares about the words and wants us to feel and understand what we are singing.

Worship God in song privately. Often I will find myself singing while driving my car, mowing the yard, taking a shower, or doing some other routine task. We can worship God in song anywhere, just as we can pray anywhere. Learn to let singing praises to God lift your spirit as it worships Him!

Sing with others. Our chief goal in singing should be to worship God, but that is not our only goal. Our singing teaches and inspires others (Colossians 3:16). It also encourages and uplifts us as we sing.

Let's make a greater commitment to worshiping God and teaching, encouraging and inspiring one another with our singing. Sing your praise to the Lord!

Talking Back

1. What role does music play in your life? What is your favorite kind of music and why?

2. Give an example when music has motivated or inspired you.

3. How would you explain to someone the reason for using only a cappella music in our church assemblies?

4. Referring to 1 Corinthians 14:15, what do you think it means to sing with our spirit and our mind?

5. What are your favorite church songs, hymns or devotional songs and why?

Exercising Your Faith

Make a list of church songs, hymns or devotional songs that are the most meaningful to you. Thank God for their influence in your life to motivate and inspire you and to worship Him.

CHAPTER 12

Giving
SUPPLYING NEEDS

A wanderer who was traveling in the mountains found a precious stone in a stream. The next day he met another traveler who was hungry, and the wanderer opened his bag to share his food. The hungry traveler saw the precious stone in the wanderer's bag, admired it, and asked the wanderer to give it to him. The wanderer did so without hesitation. The traveler left, rejoicing in his good fortune. He knew the jewel was worth enough to give him security for the rest of his life.

But a few days later he came back searching for the wanderer. When he found him, he returned the stone and said, "I have been thinking. I know how valuable this stone is, but I will give it back to you in the hope that you can give me something much more precious."

"What could that possibly be?" asked the wanderer.

"If you can," said the man, "give me what you have within you that enabled you to give me the stone."

When you give of yourself, you truly give. Ralph Waldo Emerson gave us true insight when he wrote, "Rings and jewels are not gifts, but apologies for gifts. The only true gift is a portion of thyself."

Jesus gave Himself for us at the Cross. God gave Himself to us in the sacrifice of His one and only Son. Is it too much to ask of us to give back a portion of ourselves to the Lord?

Giving of our money, our time, our talents and our energies actually is a double blessing. Not only does it benefit the recipient of our giving, but it also benefits us because Jesus said, "It is more blessed to give than to receive."

Money and giving are important parts of the Christian life – not the most important as one might assume from watching the money-grabbing, greedy religious media preachers, but important.

It may surprise you to learn that one out of every four verses in the gospel of Luke talks about money. Of the 38 parables told by Jesus, 12 deal with money. Jesus spoke about money more than He spoke about heaven and hell combined. Why? Because it is a test of our commitment to Christ.

Jesus said, "For where your treasure is, there your heart will be also" (Matthew 6:21). Here are some areas we should treasure:

Supporting the work and the ministry of the church. In the Old Testament, God's people were required to give a minimum of 10 percent (tithe) to support the temple and to do God's work. A similar general principle was commanded in the New Testament (1 Corinthians 16:1-2) and then shown by example in the church at Philippi (Philippians 4) and the Christians at Macedonia (2 Corinthians 8-9). Paul clearly taught that those who give all their time to preaching/teaching the gospel should live from the giving of fellow Christians (1 Corinthians 9:1-14; 1 Timothy 5:17). The amount of local and foreign mission work, benevolence, education and fellowship that a local congregation is able to do largely depends on the liberal giving of God's people.

Supporting the needy. Giving to people in need is a very effective way of showing the love of God to other people (Acts 4:34-37; Galatians 6:10).

Giving because of our fellowship with one another. If you are genuinely interested in fellowship with another person, you care enough to give or share with them. Financial sharing is a difficult lesson for American Christians to learn. We have been nurtured on selfishness, the me-first philosophy. We often measure the stature of a person by the amount of money and private property he has accumulated. What a distance we have come from the attitude of the early Christians toward giving and fellowship:

All the believers were together and had everything in common. Selling their possessions and goods, they gave to anyone as he had need (Acts 2:44-45).

All the believers were one in heart and mind. No one claimed that any of his possessions was his own, but they shared everything they had (Acts 4:32).

Giving because we benefit from giving. It is clear from Scripture that God often blesses us in proportion to our giving:

Give, and it will be given to you. A good measure, pressed down, shaken together and running over, will be poured into your lap. For with the measure you use, it will be measured to you (Luke 6:38).

It is more blessed to give than to receive (Acts 20:35).

Often we are the primary recipients of our own sacrificial giving.

What Is the Plan for Our Giving?

We should give regularly.

Now about the collection for God's people: Do what I told the Galatians churches to do. On the first day of every week, each one of you should set aside a sum of money in keeping with his income, saving it up, so that when I come no collections will have to be made (1 Corinthians 16:1-2).

From the beginning of its history, the church began meeting for regular worship on the first day of the week. Sunday became an appropriate and convenient time to give. Certainly we are not limited to giving only on Sundays, but it seems to be the day on which the early church collected its offerings. This allows for planned, systematic giving as opposed to unplanned, spur-of-the-moment giving.

Our giving is a personal matter. "[E]ach one of you should set aside a sum of money" (1 Corinthians 16:2). Giving is an individual, personal matter between each person and God and is not to be publicly advertised (Matthew 6:1-4).

Our giving should be in proportion to our income. We are to give in keeping with our income (1 Corinthians 16:2). Although there is no direct command about tithing (giving 10 percent of one's income) in the New Testament as in the Old

Testament, it is somewhat illogical to believe that God would expect less than 10 percent of our income under a better covenant than He did under the Old Law. If anything, it would seem that we should give more.

What Should Be Our Attitude in Giving?

We should give with love. God is very interested in why we give as well as what we give. Our motivation and sincerity in giving are ways God examines our heart:

> But just as you excel in everything – in faith, in speech, in knowledge, in complete earnestness and in your love for us – see that you also excel in this grace of giving. I am not commanding you, but I want to test the sincerity of your love by comparing it with the earnestness of others (2 Corinthians 8:7-8).

We should give cheerfully, not grudgingly. We are to avoid giving reluctantly or under compulsion. Giving should never degenerate into a guilt trip.

> Then it will be ready as a generous gift, not as one grudgingly given. Remember this: Whoever sows sparingly will also reap sparingly, and whoever sows generously will also reap generously. Each man should give what he has decided in his heart to give, not reluctantly or under compulsion, for God loves a cheerful giver (2 Corinthians 9:5-7).

We should give sacrificially. Jesus related a true incident concerning sacrificial giving:

> Jesus sat down opposite the place where the offerings were put and watched the crowd putting their money into the temple treasury. Many rich people threw in large amounts. But a poor widow came and put in two very small copper coins, worth only a fraction of a penny.
>
> Calling his disciples to him, Jesus said, "I tell you the truth, this poor widow has put more into the treasury than all the others. They all gave out of their wealth; but she,

out of her poverty, put in everything – all she had to live on" (Mark 12:41-44).

The widow could have given one of the two coins and it would have been 50 percent giving – not bad! But she gave sacrificially, putting her complete faith and trust in God. Many people will give sacrificially for a new car, house or some other luxury, but how many people ever give sacrificially to the Lord?

It is important that we obey God in the matter of giving. We often find it easy to trust God and practice what the Bible says about baptism, the church, worship and morality. But we must apply this same standard of trust and practice about giving. After all, Jesus Himself said, "It is more blessed to give than to receive."

Talking Back

1. Why do you think it has become uncomfortable or unpopular to talk about giving in church?

2. What is a tithe? Is it applicable to Christianity today?

3. Referring to 2 Corinthians 9, what attitudes must we avoid in giving? What attitudes should we have when giving?

4. What does 2 Corinthians 8:7-8 indicate is one of God's purposes for our giving? What are some other good purposes of giving?

5. Jesus said, "It is more blessed to give than to receive" (Acts 20:35). Discuss how giving can actually be more blessed than receiving. Share any examples in your life where this principle proved true.

Exercising Your Faith

Find some Christian cause you really believe in, and commit to giving to it this week. If you are unable to give money, then volunteer your time or talent.

CHAPTER 13

The Church

BE ALL YOU
CAN BE

The typical American family was driving home after church one Sunday. Dad was fussing about the sermon being too long and too boring. Mom complained about the song selection. The teenage daughter didn't like the long prayer. Grandma said she couldn't hear very well.

Eight-year-old Johnny started to complain about the lady sitting behind him who was singing off-key but instead said, "You gotta admit, it was a pretty good show for only the quarter you had to put in that plate that passed by!"

To more people than we would dare admit, attending church is like watching a show – the better the entertainment factor, the more they enjoy coming, and the less they like what they see and hear, the more they complain! But the church is far more than a show where we seek entertainment or a routine activity that leaves us complaining about some aspect of the worship service.

According to the Bible, the church is the body of Christ and the family of God.

The study of the church would be much easier if the Bible would provide a single definition of it. We could just read that definition ("The church of Christ is … "), agree to it, and never have any misunderstandings. But the Bible does not give us a precise word-for-word definition of the church. Instead, we are given word pictures to illustrate the true meaning of the church.

Above all, the church is people. It is misleading to think of buildings or programs or organizations or schools or structure as the church. The church is people, plain and simple.

Let's focus on the church of Our Lord Jesus Christ: its definition, its purpose, our obligations to it, and its personal relevance in our lives.

The Church – Its Definition

The word translated "church" comes from two Greek words: *ek*, which means out of, and *kaleo*, which means a calling. So, the church is a called-out group of believers who assemble for the purpose of carrying out God's commands and for the providing of fellowship, strength, encouragement and growth for God's people.

I am one of the ministers for the Gulf Coast congregation in Ft. Myers, Fla. To say, "I belong to the Gulf Coast Church of Christ" does not refer to the building at the corner of McGregor and Jefferson streets in Ft. Myers, but indicates, "I am a member of the assembly of believers who meet regularly in a building on the corner of McGregor and Jefferson."

A tornado or some other natural disaster could destroy the building, but the church would remain untouched because the church is the people. Wherever a congregation of Christians assemble in the world, whatever the size of the group (even if only two or three are gathered in Christ's name, Matthew 18:20), Christ is there in the midst of them, and in the truest sense, they are the church. So, the church is not a building, a structure or an organization, but it is the people, the called-out assembly of believers.

We Don't Go to Church. We Are the Church!

Several New Testament passages spell out what it means to be the church, but for the sake of time and space, we will focus on just one:

> As you come to him, the living Stone – rejected by men but chosen by God and precious to him – you also, like living stones, are being built into a spiritual house to be a holy priesthood, offering spiritual sacrifices acceptable to God through Jesus Christ. For in Scripture it says:
> "See I lay a stone in Zion, a chosen and precious cor-

nerstone, and the one who trusts in him will never be put to shame."

Now to you who believe, this stone is precious. But to those who do not believe, "The stone the builders rejected has become the capstone," and, "A stone that causes men to stumble and a rock that makes them fall." They stumble because they disobey the message – which is also what they are destined for.

But you are a chosen people, a royal priesthood, a holy nation, a people belonging to God, that you may declare the praises of him who called you out of darkness into his wonderful light. Once you were not a people, but now you are the people of God; once you had not received mercy, but now you have received mercy (1 Peter 2:4-10).

You are living stones (v. 5). We derive our life from the living Stone, Jesus Christ (v. 4). Only through Christ can we have eternal life.

You are a spiritual house (v. 5). This terminology of the church being a household or a family is also used in other passages (Ephesians 2:19; 1 Timothy 3:15). We are right, then, to call our local congregation a family, the family of God. We are born into the family by water and the Spirit at baptism (John 3:5). We eat our family meals (communion); we try to bring honor to the family name (Christian); and we are obedient to the Head of the family (Christ).

You are a holy priesthood (v. 5). All Christians are priests now with instructions to offer spiritual sacrifices.

You are a chosen people (v. 9). Just as surely as the people of Israel were God's chosen people through His covenant with them in the Old Testament, Christians are His chosen people today.

You are a royal priesthood (v. 9). In the New Testament church, every member is a priest, offering himself as a spiritual sacrifice to God (Romans 12:1; 1 Peter 2:5), just as Old Testament priests offered burnt offerings on behalf of their people. Instead of requiring the service of a priest to intercede for us, we have become priests ourselves, with Jesus interceding for us.

You are a holy nation (v. 9). As the people of Israel were holy, or set apart, to God, so the church of Jesus Christ now is sacred or holy, not bound by any racial, social or national distinctions, but sprinkled like salt around the earth to share the message of Jesus with everyone.

The Church – Its Purpose

Again, there are many passages that emphasize the purposes of the church, but we will focus on Acts 2:42-47, which outlines the purpose and program of the first church at Jerusalem:

> They devoted themselves to the apostles' teaching and to the fellowship, to the breaking of bread and to prayer. Everyone was filled with awe, and many wonders and miraculous signs were done by the apostles. All the believers were together and had everything in common. Selling their possessions and goods, they gave to anyone as he had need. Every day they continued to meet together in the temple courts. They broke bread in their homes and ate together with glad and sincere hearts, praising God and enjoying the favor of all the people. And the Lord added to their number daily those who were being saved (Acts 2:42-47).

A purpose of the church is to teach (v. 42). These new Christians wanted to learn everything they could about their Lord. The church was their primary source for learning and receiving instruction. This eagerness for knowledge and learning should be present in us today as we meet with the church.

A purpose of the church is to fellowship (v. 42). God does not want us to be a rock or an island, but a bridge and an oasis. We need others, and others need us. God made us that way (Ephesians 4:11-16). We are in fellowship with Christ and with one another as the church:

> But if we walk in the light, as he is in the light, we have fellowship with one another, and the blood of Jesus, his Son, purifies us from all sin (1 John 1:7).

A purpose of the church is communion (v. 42). As we discussed in Chapter 9, the Lord's Supper (or breaking of bread) reminds us of Jesus' sacrificial death for us on the cross. The church communes together for this memorial observance each Sunday.

A purpose of the church is prayer (v. 42). In the church assembly, in their homes and privately they talked with God, and so should we. As we meet, we pray for one another and with one another. The church is to be devoted to prayer.

A purpose of the church is to be devoted to unselfish love (vv. 44-46). They were generous and loving, taking care of one another and sharing everything in common. It is no wonder their numbers grew daily in this kind of atmosphere (v. 47).

Certainly there are other purposes of the church, but these listed in Acts 2:42-47 seem to emphasize the essentials, the basics. Concentrating on these five basic purposes of the church is a difficult task. It is so easy for the church to get sidetracked in other matters that may be good but not essential. Solid, balanced, biblical churches keep at the task of perfecting these basic purposes that were the priorities of the early church.

The Church – Our Obligations to It

As Christians, we are obligated to attend and participate in a church family. Hebrews 10:25 instructs us:

> Let us not give up meeting together, as some are in the habit of doing, but let us encourage one another.

Although this verse is well known, the preceding verse, which is often neglected, tells us why we must meet together regularly:

> And let us consider how we may spur one another on toward love and good deeds (Hebrews 10:24).

Every Christian should be faithful to attend and participate in the worship and work of the church – to praise God, to encourage others and to grow personally. Why would a true Christian want it to be any other way?

As Christians, we are obligated to give of our time, talents and money. Jesus was the perfect picture of compassion because

He was always ready to love, eager to help, and quick to act. If we wear His name, Christian, we should be like Him: self-giving, gracious and active, because, to paraphrase Oscar Hammerstein,

> A bell is not a bell till you ring it.
> A song is not a song till you sing it.
> Love is not put into your heart to stay –
> Love is only love when you give it away!

As Christians, our primary loyalty and dedication should be to Christ and His body, the church. If Christ and His church are the most important priorities for a Christian, then his or her life should be centered on Christ and the church. Jesus said,

> But seek first his kingdom and his righteousness, and all these things will be given to you as well (Matthew 6:33).

Several centuries ago in a mountain village in Europe, a wealthy man wondered what legacy he should leave to his townspeople. He decided to build them a church building. No one was permitted to see the plans or the inside of the building until it was finished. At its grand opening, the people gathered and marveled at the beauty of the new church building. Everything seemed to have been thought of and included. It was a masterpiece.

But then someone said, "Wait a minute! Where are the lamps? It is really quite dark in here. How will the church be lighted?" The wealthy builder pointed to some brackets in the walls, and then he gave each family a lamp, which they were to bring with them each time they came to worship.

"Each time you are here," the wealthy man said, 'the place where you are seated will be lighted. Each time you are not here, that place will be dark. This is to remind you that whenever you fail to come to church, some part of God's house will be dark!"

That story makes a very significant point about the importance of our loyalty and dedication to the church. The poet Edward Everett Hale put it like this:

> I am only one.
> But I am still one.
> I cannot do everything,

> But still I can do something;
> And because I cannot do everything
> I will not refuse to do the something I can do.

What if every member of your church attended the church, loved the church, served the church, and supported the church exactly as you do? What kind of church would you have?

When I was a teenager, I saw a poster that challenged my thinking and still does. It read: "If you were arrested for being a Christian, would there be enough evidence to convict you?"

Good question! Challenging question! How would you answer?

Paraphrasing that question, let me ask: "If you were arrested for being an active member of your church, would there be enough evidence to convict you?"

If not, why not?

The church is the body of Christ and the family of God. It deserves our attendance, participation, giving, loyalty and dedication. If we love Jesus, we will love His body, the church!

Talking Back

1. Play the word association game. What first comes to your mind when you hear the word "church"?

2. How would you define "church"? What are some popular misconceptions about church?

3. Of the analogies given for the church in 1 Peter 2:5-9, which is most meaningful to you and why?

4. How would you describe the primary purposes or ministries of a church?

5. Why should we feel a desire and an obligation to attend and participate in church? Why do you think so many believers neglect to attend or participate faithfully?

Exercising Your Faith

In a few words, write what your church family means to you – what you like most, what you would miss, etc. Let your writing remind you to thank God for His church, your spiritual family.

CPSIA information can be obtained at www.ICGtesting.com
Printed in the USA
LVOW081258270912

300584LV00001B/23/A